FACT OR FICTION

fact or fiction THE DILEMMA OF THE RENAISSANCE STORYTELLER

BY WILLIAM NELSON

Harvard University Press, Cambridge, Massachusetts, 1973

PREFATORY NOTE

With the permission of the publishers, I have incorporated into this book two essays originally published elsewhere. For this purpose, they have been in part rewritten and considerably reorganized. The first, entitled "The Boundaries of Fiction in the Renaissance: A Treaty between Truth and Falsehood," was read before the Tudor and Stuart Club, the Johns Hopkins University, at its annual meeting in 1967 and printed in *ELH, A Journal of English Literary History,* 36 (1969), 30–58. The second, under the title "Spenser *ludens,*" was presented at the Spenser colloquium held at St. Thomas University, Fredericton, New Brunswick, in 1969 and has since been published as part of the proceedings of that meeting (*A Theatre for Spenserians,* ed. Judith M. Kennedy and James A. Reither, University of Toronto Press, 1973). Material from these essays appears principally in Chapters I and IV, below.

CONTENTS

FACT OR FICTION

INTRODUCTION

Sir Philip Sidney says of the writer of fictions: "Though he re-count things not true, yet because he telleth them not for true, he lieth not . . . so think I none so simple would say that Aesop lied in the tales of his beasts; for who thinks that Aesop writ it for actually true were well worthy to have his name chronicled among the beasts he writeth of."[1] Truth is of many kinds, but as the word "true" is used here and as I use it throughout this study it is limited in its reference to the correspondence of a tale with things that have happened, the kind of correspondence that should obtain between the testimony of a witness in a courtroom and the events he describes. The simple challenge to which Sidney is responding asks why any mature and virtuous person should write or read fiction, that is, an account of things that never occurred.

To us as to Sidney the difference between fact and fiction seems obvious, and confusion of the two merely naïve. But the very vehemence with which Sidney repels the indictment of fic-tion as lie shows that he takes the challenge seriously. He is not alone; most of the critical essayists of the Renaissance feel constrained to deal with the accusation in one way or another. Their extraordinary sensitivity to the charge of lying is sug-gested by the hundreds of entries under the words "truth" and "falsity" in the index to Professor Weinberg's *History of Lit-erary Criticism in the Italian Renaissance*.[2] My purpose in this

1. Philip Sidney, *An Apology for Poetry*, ed. Geoffrey Shepherd (London, T. Nelson, 1965), p. 124.
2. Bernard Weinberg, *History of Literary Criticism in the Italian Renaissance* (Chicago, University of Chicago Press, 1961).

book is to trace the history of that defensive attitude, to examine the reasons for it, and to consider its consequences for the nature and tone of sixteenth- and seventeenth-century fictitious narrative, whether in prose or in verse. To the extent that the effort succeeds, it should aid an appreciation of those stories in a manner appropriate to the period in which they were written, apart from conceptions bred in the modern reader by the literary traditions with which he is most familiar, particularly the massive tradition of the serious novel. And although the approach is different in direction from the search for the "antecedents" of the novel, it may, nevertheless, reveal some of the forces which determined the nature of that genre itself.

Concern for the difference between fiction and the false tale which is told "for true" depends upon the importance attached to historical truth. When from a knowledge of what actually happened in the past there flow significant consequences—the inheritance of property, the conviction of the accused, the salvation of the soul—historical truth must inevitably be regarded as precious. Even when there are no such consequences a detected lie is doubtless embarrassing. But truth is by no means always ascertainable, nor is it always of practical importance to ascertain it—witness the rather contemptuous use of the word "academic" as applied to that unremitting search for truth to which universities are supposed to be dedicated. Travelers, fishermen, and politicians proverbially find truth for its own sake less valuable than other considerations. If "story" (in any of its diverse senses) is esteemed primarily for edification, entertainment, or some other purpose, the question of its verity may not arise at all, and in that case there is no need to differentiate between fiction and lie.

The classical world seems not to have been much concerned with the truth about the past, however deeply its philosophers probed the nature of moral and philosophical truths. Professor Ben Edwin Perry says, "For [the ancients] the world was primarily a world of ideas, which could be put to practical use in the instruction and edification of living men, rather than a world of facts valued only as such, and thereby useless. What moral or spiritual good is there in a mere fact? On some occasions the ancients became antiquarians and were at pains to distinguish what was probably true in the distant past from what was mythical and false; but this was not their habitual way of looking at traditional data, and least of all when they were concerned with *belles lettres*. With all his critical zeal, not even Thucydides challenges the historical reality of Deucalion and the patently eponymous Hellen; and from the Greek poetical point of view (which was that of drama and romance) Inachus, Candaules, Xerxes, Alcibiades, Ninus, Nireus, and Daphnis are alike historical and belong in the same category."[3]

Poetry, to be sure, enjoyed greater license than prose. As Hesiod, in shepherd's guise tending his flock on Mount Parnassus, learned from the Muses themselves,

> we know how to say many false things
> that seem like true sayings
> but we know also how to speak the truth
> when we wish to.[4]

Though Socrates banned poets from his Republic because they could not or would not tell the truth, he nevertheless urged that the children of the commonwealth be told such tales as would make them believe that no citizen had ever quarreled with another. Aristotle described poets and dramatists as skillful liars, but rather approved than condemned them. He not only recognized the legitimacy of invented story, but he also insisted that it was the necessary and essential ingredient of the narrative poem and the drama and urged the importance of verisimili-

3. Ben Edwin Perry, *The Ancient Romances* (Berkeley and Los Angeles, University of California Press, 1967), pp. 77–78.
4. Hesiod, *Theogony*, 27, tr. R. Lattimore.

3

tude—the primary characteristic of a successful lie—as a quality of good poetry. Strabo thought it absurd of Eratosthenes to criticize Homer for his fictions; "Homer [was] wont to add a mythical element to actual occurrences, thus giving flavour and adornment to his style; but he has the same end in view as the historian or the person who narrates facts. So, for instance, he took the Trojan war, an historical fact, and decked it out with his myths and he did the same in the case of the wanderings of Odysseus; but to hang an empty story of marvels on something wholly untrue is not Homer's way of doing things. For it occurs to us at once, doubtless, that a man will lie more plausibly if he will mix in some actual truth . . ."[5] It was reported to Cicero that some people criticized his "Marius" (the poem is lost) because much of it appeared to be fictional. Since he was dealing with recent events and with a native of Arpinium, they demanded that he stick to the truth. His answer was like that of Strabo: "My dear Titus, those 'certain persons' whom you mention display their ignorance by demanding in such a matter the kind of truthfulness expected of a witness in court rather than of a poet. No doubt these same people believe that Numa talked with Egeria, and that the cap was placed on Tarquinius' head by the eagle."[6] In sum, as Plutarch put it, poetry was an art "not greatly concerned with truth."[7]

Nor did antiquity condemn history or biography if it included that which was not true. The idea that historians should tell the truth was expressed from time to time, and in the passage immediately following his defence of "Marius" Cicero distinguished between history and poetry on the ground that the

5. Strabo, I.2.9, tr. Horace L. Jones (Loeb edition). Eratosthenes had rejected the identification of Scylla and Charybdis with the Strait of Messina: "It is useless to look for the scenes of the wanderings of Odysseus. You will find those places when you find the man who stitched together the bag of winds" (34.2.11, tr. Bury).
6. Cicero, *De legibus*, I.i.4, tr. C. W. Keyes (Loeb edition).
7. Plutarch, *Moralia* (On Reading Poetry), 17.

former was to be judged by the standard of verity, the latter by the pleasure it gave. He pointed out, however, that there were innumerable fabulous tales in the works of Herodotus, the father of history, and in those of Theopompus. His own sense of the requirements of history was not so precise as to keep him from urging his friend Lucceius to write his biography with such embellishment as would make it more admirable, even at the cost of deviating from the truth.[8] In practice, classical historians and biographers varied widely, some writers leaning toward a respect for the verifiable, others given to interesting anecdotes, decoration, invention. There were, no doubt, impostors who forged genealogies and falsely documented historical accounts with intent to deceive. But the question of historical truth does not appear to have been an urgent one. Seneca says, mockingly, "Who ever demanded affidavits from a historian?"[9]

The effect of this permissive attitude was to assimilate fiction to the general category of story, a category which included among its varieties both invented tales and whatever was told "for true," whether true or not. Cicero classified *fabula, historia,* and *argumentum* as a single species of one kind of *narratio. Fabula* he defined as that which was neither true nor verisimilar; *historia,* the account of things done in the remote past; *argumentum,* a fictional but nevertheless possible action, like that of comedy.[10] The fourth-century Vergilian commentator Servius identified *historia* with *argumentum.* Both kinds of tale recounted things that accorded with nature, whether or not they actually did happen; such was the story of Phaedra. *Fabula,* which also might or might not be true, differed from *historia* because the events were contrary to nature, as in the case

8. Cicero, *Ad familiares,* V.xii.3.
9. Seneca, *Apocolococyntosis,* in *The Satire of Seneca,* tr. Allan P. Ball (New York, Columbia University Press, 1902), p. 132.
10. Cicero, *De inventione,* I.27ff.; see also *Ad Herennium,* I.8.13, and Quintilian, II.iv.2.

of Pasiphae.[11] Such analyses rendered the differences in verity among the kinds of story of little importance in comparison to their similarity in rhetorical function. As with a circumstantial anecdote told by a chance traveling companion, what mattered was not whether the tale was true, or partly true, or not true at all, but whether it was edifying or amusing.

The problem which so preoccupied the literary criticism of the Renaissance had its roots in the rejection of this way of thinking. If Plutarch is to be trusted, that wise lawgiver of Athens, Solon, would have none of it. In those days, Plutarch says, the performing of tragedies was in its infancy. "Solon, being naturally desirous to hear and to learn, and by reason of his age seeking to pass his time away in sports, in music, and making good cheer more than ever he did: went one day to see Thespis, who played a part himself, as the old fashion of the poets was, and after the play was ended, he called him to him, and asked him: if he were not ashamed to lie so openly in the face of the world. Thespis answered him, that it was not material to do or say any such things, considering all was but in sport. Then Solon beating the ground with his staff he had in his hand: But if we commend lying in sport (quoth he) we shall find it afterward in good earnest, in all our bargains and dealings."[12] In his simple wisdom, Solon refuses to distinguish between lying as deception and lying as something other than historical truth. Solon does not argue, with Plato, that a poet is incapable of representing undistorted truth; nor does he, like Plato, condemn the content and tone of some fiction because it stirs up harmful emotions and so leads to the imitation of immoral acts. For Solon, a fiction is a lie and a lie is per se evil.

11. *Servii grammatici qui feruntur in Vergilii carmina commentarii,* ed. G. Thilo and H. Hagen (Leipzig, B. G. Teubner, 1923), on *Aeneid,* I.235 (239): "Et sciendum est, inter fabulam et argumentum, hoc est historiam, hoc interesse, quod fabula est dicta res contra naturam, siue facta siue non facta, ut de Pasiphae, historia est quicquid secundum naturam dicitur, siue factum siue non factum, ut de Phaedra."
12. Plutarch, *Life of Solon,* 29.6, tr. Sir Thomas North.

Or, to put it another way, there is no such thing as fiction for him; there is only history in the sense of *res gestae*, and history must be either true or false. That position could still be taken as late as the Renaissance. Since Thomas More had written the false tale of *Utopia,* his opponents said, he was manifestly a liar. Who then could believe him when he asserted the existence of purgatory or when he declared that the Protestant Richard Hunne was not murdered by his jailers but committed suicide?[13]

I suspect that Plutarch's anecdote is itself a fiction, for the moral indignation he ascribes to Solon is typical neither of the theory nor of the practice of the classical world. It is, however, symptomatic of an increasing concern with the truth of the past which manifests itself in the early centuries of the Christian era. Although this concern appears both in pagan and in Christian writers, the Hebraic tradition surely gave force to the idea that it was important to distinguish the veritable past from falsehood and fiction. The narrative mode of the Testaments, Erich Auerbach points out, is radically different from that of Homer: the Greek requires no belief, the Hebrew demands it.[14] It did not much matter to the Greeks whether Iphigenia was sacrificed by Agamemnon or miraculously preserved; it mattered a great deal to Christians that Jesus did not die on the cross. When the *Odyssey* and the *Aeneid* were read as if they, like the Bible, were told "for true," they became not merely lies but, since they ascribed divine powers to Zeus and to Venus, damnable lies. So the fathers of the Church described them.

The division of history into true and false associated fiction

13. See Rainer Pineas, "Thomas More's 'Utopia' and Protestant Polemics," *Renaissance News,* XVII (1964), 197–201.

14. Erich Auerbach, *Mimesis, The Representation of Reality in Western Literature,* tr. Willard Trask (Princeton, N.J., Princeton University Press, 1953), pp. 10–12. Compare Dante, *Paradiso,* XXIV, 103–105:

Risposto fummi: "Di', chi t'assicura
   che quell' opere fosser? Quel medesmo
   che vuol provarsi, non altri, il ti giura."

with the latter and infected it with its moral stain. To free himself from the charge of lying the storyteller had recourse to either of two alternatives. He might brazen it out by insisting that his fiction was no fiction at all but true history, derived from authentic sources and based on the observation of reliable witnesses. If he seriously wished to convince a sophisticated audience of this, he must avoid whatever might damage the credibility of the story: impossible or improbable actions, conflict with known truth, artistic devices associated with the lying poetry of the ancients. The other course was overt or tacit admission that the story was indeed fiction and therefore not subject to judgment as to whether it was historically true or false. Such an admission might be made by a patently jocular claim to historical truth or by the obvious difference of the tale from history. Differences now obvious to us, however, have not always been so. Before the conventionalizing of the novel the signs by which we readily distinguish fiction from nonfiction— place on library shelves, format, style—were not available, so that only the quite incredible tale could be free from confusion with historical report. Furthermore, admittedly invented story had to find its raison d'être on grounds other than those which gave true history its value.

The great mass of Renaissance literary criticism, so ably analyzed by Spingarn, Weinberg, Hathaway, and others, was largely devoted to the definition and justification of fictitious narrative, usually identified with "poetry." Much of the effort defended the proposition that though fiction was not the truth of history it was nevertheless truth in some other, more profound sense. Throughout this voluminous literature of apology, the reader senses a continuing and never fully resolved struggle against a stubborn conviction that true report was superior to any imitation of it, that despite the claims of invented narrative to moral, religious, or philosophical verity and despite the example of the great poems of antiquity fiction remained no more than a counterfeit of reality, delightful perhaps and suitable for recreation but not for the mature attention of grown men. That conviction colored the attitude of authors and audiences of the sixteenth and seventeenth centuries and profoundly affected the nature and tone of the stories they wrote and read. In the critical treatises the sense of doubt about the legitimacy and value of fiction appears principally in the form of attempts to allay it based upon reason and the authority of the ancients. It is more immediately manifest in the prefaces and apologies which introduce many of the fictions of the period because they present the author or translator as he wished to appear to his readers and so reflect his understanding of their tastes and prejudices. From these, therefore, and from the stories themselves I have drawn much of my evidence.

The first chapter of this book is concerned with the slow and uneven process, beginning in late classical times, by which fiction came to be separated from the category of history; the second, with the attempt to define the boundaries of fiction and to justify it. The remainder of the study has as its subject the ways in which storytellers of the sixteenth and seventeenth centuries responded to the notion that invented narrative was at best a waste of time. Chapters III and IV consider the approach which justified it as a concession to human weakness, defensible either because it provided recreation or because it might be made to serve as a vehicle for matter of substance. I have chosen *The Faerie Queene* to illustrate the kind of misapprehension of tone which results from attending to the narrative plot of a great Renaissance work with the seriousness suggested by Aristotle's dictum that the story is the "soul" of a tragedy or epic poem. Finally, Chapter V examines the tendency of storytellers, notably in the seventeenth century, to deny their art of "making," that is, to reject fiction by asserting that their tales were not fiction but true as history is true.

i

FROM FRAUD TO FICTION

When the easy classical acceptance of accounts of the past that are mixed with what might be imagined about the past begins to be challenged, the problem of the legitimacy of fiction presents itself. There are signs in the first centuries of the Christian era of such a change in attitude, a growing recognition that some people thought that true and false history ought to be distinguished and that the latter kind was reprehensible. Seneca plays with the possibility. His *Apocolococyntosis*, that is, "the making of a pumpkin" out of the deceased Emperor Claudius, tells of the attempt of that bad ruler to enter heaven and of his final disposition in Hades. The author declares: "I shall tell the unvarnished truth. If anybody asks me where I got my information, I say at once, I'll not answer if I don't want to . . . Still, if I must produce my authority, apply to the man who saw Drusilla [that is, the incestuous sister of the Emperor Caligula] going heavenward; he will say he saw Claudius limping along in the same direction."[1]

Seneca's joke declares that his story is as true as the tale of Drusilla's deification, his fiction as palpable as the imperial lie. Lucian is similarly jocular in his preface to *A True History*, the tale of his adventures beyond the Pillars of Hercules and in outer space. He indicts three storytellers in particular as outrageous liars: Homer's Odysseus, the historian Ctesias, and Iambulus, author of a traveler's tale. This last describes an island, far to the south, whose inhabitants have divided tongues so that

---

1. *The Satire of Seneca,* tr. Allan P. Ball (New York, Columbia University Press, 1902), p. 132.

they can imitate the calls of birds and carry on two conversations at once. The inventions of Ctesias are equally improbable but less entertaining. As for Odysseus, Lucian comments on his stories of bags full of wind, one-eyed giants, and potions that transform men into beasts: "He evidently thought the Phaeacians were fools enough to believe anything . . . My chief reaction is astonishment—that anyone should tell such lies and expect to get away with it."[2]

Lucian is doubtless only pretending to take these stories as outrageous lies rather than as entertainments. Indeed, he declares that, while Iambulus' account is obviously quite untrue, it makes a very good story. Nevertheless, he takes the position that a tale must be judged true or false, the storyteller an honest historian or a liar. And one of the last representatives of pagan culture, the Emperor Julian, soberly expresses a similar view: "It would be fitting for us to make acquaintance with those histories which are written about deeds actually done in the past; but we must deprecate those fictions put forth by previous writers in the form of history, that is, love stories and, in a word, all such stuff."[3]

While agreeing in general with this deprecation, postclassical authorities, both pagan and Christian, find it possible to defend certain kinds of invented tale on the ground that they are really true after all, true, that is, allegorically or euhemeristically. Macrobius feels called upon to respond to the scolding of Plato by the Epicurean Colotes. He reports that Colotes said about the myth of Er: "If you wished to impart to us a conception of the heavenly realms and reveal the condition of souls, why did you not do so in a simple and straightforward manner

2. Lucian, *A True History*, tr. Paul Turner (Bloomington, Indiana University Press, 1958). See also George H. Nadel, "Philosophy of History before Historicism," *History and Theory*, III (1964), 303–304.

3. Quoted by Perry, *The Ancient Romances*, p. 78, from Julian, *Epist. 89*, 301b.

instead of defiling the very portals of truth with imaginary character, event, and setting, in a vile imitation of a playwright?" Macrobius grants that fiction which delight only—the comedies of Menander and his followers, the tales of Petronius Arbiter and Apuleius—should be relegated to children's nurseries, but Platonic myths are of another character: "a decent and dignified conception of holy truths, with respectable events and characters . . . presented beneath a modest veil of allegory."[4]

This limitation of defensible fiction to veiled truth resembles the position taken by the champions of Christianity, Lactantius and St. Augustine. Lactantius wishes to turn the pagans against themselves by proving from their own stories that their gods were licentious and evil men. He will not allow his opponents to dismiss those stories as poetic figments. Such interpretation depends upon a misunderstanding of poetic license: "The poet's function consists in this, that those things which were actually performed he may transfer with some graceful converse into other appearances by means of figurative language. But to feign the whole account which you relate—that is to be a fool and a liar instead of a poet." As illustration of the truth of poetic fiction he cites the story of Jupiter's seduction of Danae, the shower of gold being merely a figure of speech for the riches by which a man tempted a girl from her chastity.[5] In a comment on Luke 24:28 a similar argument provides St. Augustine with an answer to the charge that Christ lied. The Biblical occasion is the appearance of the risen Christ to Cleopas and another: "And they drew nigh unto the village, whither they went: and he made as though [finxit] he would

4. Macrobius, *In somnium Scipionis*, II.3–17, in *Commentary on the Dream of Scipio*, tr. W. H. Stahl, Records of Civilization, Sources and Studies, Number XLVIII (New York, Columbia University Press, 1952).

5. Lactantius, *The Divine Institutes*, I.11, tr. Sister Mary Francis McDonald (Washington, D.C., Catholic University of America Press, 1964).

have gone further." Augustine explains, "What is written concerning the Lord *Finxit se longius ire* does not pertain to a lie. For not everything that we make up [*fingimus*] is a lie: but when we make up that which signifies nothing, then it is a lie. When, however, our fiction is related to a certain signification it is not a lie but in some way a figure of truth. Otherwise everything said figuratively by wise and holy men, or even by the Lord himself, will be reckoned a lie since by customary understanding truth does not abide in such discourse." Augustine then points to the story of the prodigal son as an example of fictional hiding, or rather expressing, of profound truth.[6]

Elsewhere, Augustine appears to tolerate, if not approve, stories that are so patently false that they cannot deceive. As an instance he cites the tale of Medea flying, quoting for evidence of its incredibility the verse that Cicero had used to illustrate the meaning of the term *fabula*:

> Angues ingentes alites junctos jugo[7]
> (Great winged serpents attached to the yoke)

And in the *Confessions* he protests that incredible tales and poems from which true instruction can be extracted are less noxious than the fabrications of the Manichaeans: "For verses and poems I can turn into true food, but the 'Medea flying,' though I sang, I maintained it not; though I heard it sung, I believed it not; but those [heretical] things I did believe.[8]

The curious consequence of this rejection of stories that may mislead is a rejection of the verisimilar as a narrative mode. For if a tale resembles the truth—takes the form of history— it must be judged as history. The only kind of narrative that can escape such judgment is, like those of Seneca and Lucian and the story of the flying Medea, so far beyond the bounds of

6. Augustine, 2 *quaest, Evangel., quaest. 51,* in Migne, *Patrologiae cursus, Series Latina,* XXXV, col. 1362.
7. Augustine, *Soliloquia,* II.xv.29.
8. Augustine, *Confessions,* III.6.11, tr. J. K. Pilkington.

possibility that not even a simpleton could think it history. This is explicitly the judgment of the sage-magician Apollonius of Tyana as reported in the biography by Philostratus (third century our era). Apollonius asks his disciple Menippus to compare Aesop's fables with the compositions of the "poets." Menippus prefers the latter "because they are represented in the poems as having taken place," while beast fables are "nonsense only fit to be swallowed by old women and children." Apollonius holds the contrary opinion. Aesop, he declares, "was really more attached to truth than the poets are; for the latter do violence to their own stories in order to make them probable; but he by announcing a story which everyone knows not to be true, told the truth by the very fact that he did not claim to be relating real events. And the poet, after telling his story, leaves a healthy-minded reader cudgelling his brains to know whether it really happened; whereas one who, like Aesop, tells a story which is false and does not pretend to be anything else, merely investing it with a good moral, shows that he has made use of the falsehood merely for its utility to his audience."[9] For Apollonius, then, only the kind of story which so completely lacks verisimilitude that nobody can be deceived by it is an acceptable fiction.

The period which is marked by this growing fear of being deceived is marked also by the appearance of a kind of narrative which is indeed fraudulent, fiction which pretends most energetically to be authentic history and not fiction at all. Some stories of the time, to be sure, make no such pretense. Apuleius forthrightly describes his *Golden Ass* as a Milesian tale, what the English of a later age would call a tale of Robin Hood. *Clitophon and Leucippe* and other so-called Greek romances vaguely suggest that they are historical narrations, but I cannot suppose that deception was intended or had effect. In con-

9. *The Life of Apollonius of Tyana,* V.14, tr. F. C. Conybeare (London, Heinemann, 1912), I, 493–495.

trast, the stories of the Trojan war attributed to Dictys the Cretan and Dares the Phrygian can be described only as frauds. The former tale which dates in fact from the third century is said to have been written on linden tablets in Phoenician characters by a participant in the battle. He returned to Crete after the war ended and in his old age provided that the history be buried with him. Centuries later, in the time of the Emperor Nero, a violent earthquake opened the vault. Certain peasants found the document and took it to their landlord who took it to the imperial governor who presented it to the emperor at whose instance it was translated into Greek and then into Latin.[10] Fragments of a Greek version have been discovered, but the story is, in truth, merely a conflation of classical accounts made more like history by the elimination of the supernatural. The recovery of the history of Dares the Phrygian required nothing so catastrophic as an earthquake, but its credentials are as detailed and as fraudulent as those of Dictys. In a letter purporting to be addressed to the historian Sallust a writer using the name of the historian Cornelius Nepos declares that he has found the document in Athens, in Dares' own hand, and has translated it into Latin. He remarks on the evident superiority in truthfulness of this report by an eyewitness over the account of Homer who, by his own admission, lived many years after the battle. Furthermore, Dares writes of no palpable absurdities such as gods joining with men in battlefield melees.[11] Even more elaborate documentation is provided for the tale entitled *Wonders beyond Thule*, first discovered (so it is said) in a subterranean vault by some soldiers of Alexander during the conquest of Tyre and much later divulged to the world by one Antonius Diogenes.

Wonders beyond Thule is known to us only from a summary

10. Dictys Cretensis and Dares Phrygius, *The Trojan War: the Chronicles of Dictys of Crete and Dares the Phrygian*, tr. R. M. Frazer (Bloomington, Indiana University Press, 1966), pp. 20–21.
11. *Ibid.*, p. 133.

of its contents by Photius, a Greek scholar of the ninth century.[12] It may be that its author expected his readers to be entertained rather than fooled by the story of its provenance. Perhaps the compilers of the Dictys and Dares narratives hoped for some reward, financial or other, for their "discoveries." At this distance their motives are difficult to assess. But the purpose animating the authors of a particular kind of tale, increasingly common from the third century on, is both powerful and transparent. The postclassical age bubbled volcanically with new religions, sects, and cults, and Christianity, in particular, based its claim to credence on testamentary evidence supplied by irreproachable witnesses. The evangelists had given mutually corroborating testimony concerning certain marvelous events of no great antiquity; the world was divided between those who believed and those who did not. A mass of additions to the Biblical base appeared: gospels, epistles, visions, and autobiographical narratives attributed to the Old Testament fathers and prophets, to the apostles, to Joseph, his son James, Mary, and to Jesus himself. Typically, the purpose of these writings was to reinforce the faith of believers and to convert or controvert others. A few examples, chosen almost at random, will show the kind of technique employed.

Most of the characteristics of this "historical" genre appear in an *Apocalypse of Paul* which was composed (or, if the text is to be believed, discovered) in the third century:

In the consulate of Theodosius Augustus the younger and Cynegius, a certain honourable man then dwelling at Tarsus, in the house which had been the house of Saint Paul, an angel appeared unto him by night and gave him a revelation, saying that he should break up the foundation of the house and publish what he found; but he thought this to be a lying vision.

12. Photius, *Bibliothèque,* cod. 166, ed. and tr. by René Henry (Paris, Société d'édition "Les Belles lettres," 1959–1967), II, 140ff. Photius himself describes the story as "incredible and mendacious" (p. 147).

But a third time the angel came, and scourged him and com-
pelled him to break up the foundation. And he dug, and found
a box of marble inscribed upon the sides; therein was the revelation of Saint Paul, and his shoes wherein he walked when he
taught the word of God. But he feared to open that box and
brought it to the judge; and the judge took it, sealed as it was
with lead, and sent it to the emperor Theodosius, fearing that
it might be something strange; and the emperor when he received it, opened it and found the revelation of Saint Paul. A
copy thereof he sent to Jerusalem, and the original he kept
with him.[13]

Sometimes the testament, instead of being buried in a marble box, has been preserved by a dedicated priesthood from
contamination by the vulgar, or by heretics. The preservation
accounts for the gap in time between the events narrated and
their publication. This is the case with that strange theological
adventure story about the confrontation of St. Peter and Simon
Magus called *The Recognitions of Clement*—the Clement re-
puted to be Peter's successor to the see of Rome. A similar
device is used to win credence for the *Liber de Infantia,* or
Gospel of Pseudo-Matthew. A letter attributed to St. Jerome
which appears in some of the manuscripts explains that Matthew had not intended the work for general circulation: "For
had it not been somewhat secret, he would no doubt have
added it to the Gospel which he published. But in fact he composed this book to be locked up in Hebrew letters, and so far
refrained from publishing it that even now the book, written in
Hebrew letters with his own hand, is kept by certain religious
men who have received it from their predecessors through a
long course of time." Nevertheless, the letter continues, a
Manichaean named Leucius has published it in such manner
as to afford not edification but perdition. Jerome therefore
translates, presumably from the holograph, the words of an

13. Montague Rhodes James, *The Apocryphal New Testament*
(Oxford, Eng., Clarendon Press, 1924), p. 526.

apostle and evangelist, not in order to add to the canonical writings but in order to confute heresy.[14]

In their competition for the minds of men the inventors of these tales strained their imaginations to provide the most authoritative and circumstantial proof of their historicity. The story of the death of Joseph warranted belief because it was said to have been told by Christ Himself to the apostles on Mount Olivet, then written down by them, and laid up in the library at Jerusalem.[15] The *Gospel of Nicodemus* was described as having been discovered by Ananias the Protector, of praetorian rank, who sought out the memorials that the Jews had deposited with Pontius Pilate. He translated them from Hebrew into Greek in the reign of Lord Flavius Theodosius, in the seventeenth year, and of Flavius Valentinus the sixth, in the ninth indiction. In the gospel itself, we are told that Karinus and Leucius, resurrected from the dead, were required to write out the story of their experiences. They did so separately, and when they were done they delivered their volumes to different elders. On comparison, the two accounts were found to be exactly the same, differing not even by a letter.[16] Perhaps the most overwhelming authority cited was that for a testament decribed by Hippolytus. This revelation was vouchsafed to one Elchasai in the town of Serai, in Parthia, by an angel 96 miles high, 16 miles broad, and 24 miles from shoulder to shoulder. The tracks of his feet were 14 miles long, 6 miles wide, and 2 miles deep. He was the Son of God, and he was accompanied by the female Holy Spirit, of the same dimensions.[17]

Credibility for these narratives was sought not only by de-

14. *Ibid.*, p. 71.
15. *Ibid.*, p. 84.
16. *Ibid.*, pp. 95, 122–123.
17. Reported by Hippolytus, *Philosophumena* IX.8. See the *Ante-Nicene Fathers*, ed. Alexander Roberts and James Donaldson, American reprint of the Edinburgh edition (New York, The Christian Literature Company, 1925), V, 131ff. Hippolytus's account may be a mockery of the original which is not extant.

tailed documentation of their provenance but also by the circumstantial character of the tales themselves. The author of the gospel attributed to Matthew hoped that he would quench any lingering doubts as to that critical point of the faith, the virgin birth, by telling of the gynecological examination performed on Mary after the nativity by two skeptical and reputable midwives (one is named Salome, the other Zelomi: two witnesses are better than one). In punishment for her doubt Salome's hand withers, but it is restored when an angel leads her to touch the fringe of the Infant's clothing.[18] The same desire to carry conviction which leads to such crudities also produced imaginative writing of great vividness. The *Book of James* or *Protevangelium* tells of the moment of Christ's birth as Joseph saw it:

Now I Joseph was walking, and I walked not. And I looked up to the air and saw the air in amazement. And I looked up unto the pole of the heaven and saw it standing still, and the fowls of the heaven without motion. And I looked upon the earth and saw a dish set, and workmen lying by it, and their hands were in the dish: and they that were chewing chewed not, and they that were lifting the food lifted it not, and they that put it to their mouth put it not thereto, but the faces of all of them were looking upward. And behold there were sheep being driven, and they went not forward but stood still; and the shepherd lifted his hand to smite them with his staff, and his hand remained up. And I looked upon the stream of the river and saw the mouths of the kids upon the water and they drank not. And of a sudden all things moved onward in their course.[19]

The circumstantial documentation of works like these was received with varying degrees of skepticism. Although Church councils declared the *Apocalypse of Paul*, the *Gospel of Nicodemus*, and the *Recognitions of Clement* apocryphal, they con-

18. *The Gospel of Pseudo-Matthew*, in *Ante-Nicene Fathers*, VIII, 374–375.
19. James, *The Apocryphal New Testament*, p. 46.

tinued to be read and copied throughout the Middle Ages; sometimes they seem to be better known than Scripture itself. Their acceptance in this sense depends upon the special position of the canonical books of the Bible. Those indeed must be taken as articles of faith; they constitute history itself, the touchstone by which all other tales of the past must be tested. Other histories, whatever their nature, either conflict or do not conflict with Truth. If they do, they are lies; if they do not, they may be read without danger to the soul, perhaps with profit. If the story is not demonstrably false, therefore, judgment as to its acceptablity rests upon its religious and moral value. The attitude may be represented by another letter attributed to Jerome which is found in some manuscripts as preface to the *Gospel of the Pseudo-Matthew:*

I shall be careful to translate it word for word as it is in the Hebrew, inasmuch as it appears that the holy evangelist Matthew composed this same book and prefixed it, concealed as it was in Hebrew letters, to his Gospel. The truth of this statement I leave to the author of the preface and the faith of the writer; for myself, while pronouncing it doubtful, I do not affirm that it is clearly false. This, however, I say boldly, that I believe none of the faithful will deny that, whether this story be true or invented by some one, great miracles preceded the holy birth of Mary, and yet greater ones followed upon it; and therefore this can be believed and read with intact faith and without peril to the soul, by those who believe that God is able to do such things.[20]

This approaches a defense of fiction on the ground that it provides moral or religious instruction. Yet it is not such a defense, for it concerns not avowed fiction but a historical narrative of hidden or uncertain provenance, one which may be true after all. The tale is to be read as an account of the past, though not *the* account of the past—only the Bible falls into the latter category.

20. *Ibid.,* p. 72.

The apocryphal tales created a substantial precedent for a kind of imaginative literature which was presented not as fiction but as documented history. A great mass of medieval narrative, both religious and secular, is in this quasi-historical mode.[21] From late classical times and throughout the Middle Ages storytellers assert, often with great energy and circumstance, that their narratives are historically true, based on the most reliable of authorities. In certain kinds of tale, like the dream vision and the animal fable, the pretense is either very thin or nonexistent; the detachment of such stories from reality puts them outside the realm of history, as the sage Apollonius is said to have said. But typically, the medieval story is a historical report the credibility of which is reinforced by its venerable antiquity, by the circumstantial nature of its testimony, and by the unimpeachable character of its author. The discovery of an old book containing such a report is a remarkably common device: the book has lain hidden for a long time; it was buried, or lost, or closely guarded. The discovery is often said to have been aided or witnessed or corroborated by some responsible person, an emperor, an abbot, or an archdeacon. The book is found in a tomb, under the high altar of a monastery, in the ruins of the ancient city of Verulam, in Arthur's burial place of Avalon, in the abbey church of St. Denys. It may be written in an exotic language or in a strange script: Phoenician, Hebrew, Trojan, ancient British, or, vaguely, heathen. It is partially destroyed or faded or difficult to decipher. Sometimes the discoverer translates it in full; sometimes he summarizes it; sometimes he supplements it from other reli-

21. See the important essay by Friedrich Wilhelm, "Ueber fabulistische quellenangaben," in *Beiträge zur Geschichte der deutschen Sprache und Literatur*, XXXIII (Halle, M. Niemeyer, 1908), 24–39. See also A. J. Tieje, "The Critical Heritage of Fiction in 1579," *Englische Studien*, XLVII (1913–14), 415–447; and H. L. Levy, " 'As myn auctour seyth,' " *Medium Aevum*, XII (1945), 24–39.

able sources. It is impossible to test the accuracy of these prefatory statements for somehow the long lost book rarely turns up again. We may be told why: the life of St. Alban written in the "British" tongue, which was found during an excavation of the ancient city of Verulam, disintegrated into dust immediately after it was copied.[22]

In fact, the medieval storyteller, posing as historian, probably did get his tale out of a book, or from somebody else's telling. He felt free to translate verbatim, to render into verse that which was prose and into prose that which was verse. He was not at all ashamed to take his matter from another; indeed, like a proper historian, he insisted that he did so. But, typically, he denied that he had invented anything at all, even when he had invented a great deal. And when he cited his authority it was often not the true source but a document no one has been able to discover. Since much medieval literature is lost, we may in some cases be maligning a storyteller who claims to be translating a work we cannot find and therefore think imaginary. But the ubiquity of the practice of false documentation is beyond question. It is necessary only to sample the main branches of medieval narratives: the saints' legends and the "matters" of Troy, of France, and of Britain.

Even the casual reader of medieval legendaries will recognize both the fictional character of many of the saints' lives and the spuriousness of the documentation with which they are provided. Entombed manuscripts and unvarnished eyewitness reports abound. The widely popular account of Barlaam and Josaphat is in fact a "borrowing" from the life of Buddha. But it is said to be a relation to St. John of Damascus (an eighth-century Syrian monk) by some pious Ethiopians who had found it engraved on tablets. The legend of St. Ephysius of Cagliari is certainly a fabrication since it closely imitates a version of the older legend of St. Procopius. Never-

22. Wilhelm, "Ueber fabulistische quellenangaben," pp. 322-323.

theless, its author insists that he, the presbyter Marcus, was a witness to the passion from beginning to end, and that he has described the events "fideliter veraciterque." The learned Bollandist Father Delehaye remarks sadly, "This declaration does not allow us to believe for an instant in the good faith of the biographer of St. Ephysius."[23] As Delehaye points out, the hagiographers customarily borrowed the stories of other saints, expanded and decorated them, and invented new tales in order to edify morally or to honor particular localities, families, or religious orders. And, customarily, they documented their inventions as sober history.

The Troy stories of the Middle Ages were based not upon Homer, Vergil, and Ovid, who were thought to be ill-informed historians and liars as well, but upon the eyewitness accounts of Dictys the Cretan and Dares the Phrygian. The Dictys-Dares tradition was carried on by Benoît de St. Maur's twelfth-century *Roman de Troie* and Guido de Columnis' *Historia destructionis Troiae*, a century later. Benoît honestly cites Dares as his source. But he insists that he has added nothing whatever: "I shall follow the Latin to the letter. I shall put in nothing but as I find it written. Nor do I say or add any good saying, even had I the skill, but I shall follow my matter."[24] In fact, he invents many characters and episodes; he is the creator, for example, of the story of Troilus and Briseida which eventually became Boccaccio's *Filostrato* and Chaucer's *Troilus and Criseyde*—the tale which Chaucer borrowed from Boccaccio but said he had translated from a nonexistent history by one Lollius. Guido is even more unreliable than Benoît who was his principal source. He does not mention Benoît at all. Instead, Guido begins with a eulogy of true history which preserves the deeds of the ancients from the destruction of time.

23. Hippolyte Delehaye, *Les Légendes Hagiographiques* (Brussels, Société des Bollandistes, 1955), p. 136.
24. *Bénoit de Sainte-More et Le Roman de Troie*, ed. A. Joly (Paris, 1871), II, 26–27.

He then criticizes Homer and his followers, Vergil and Ovid, as superstitious and untrustworthy. Dictys and Dares are the proper authorities, their faithful accounts having been found written in their own hands in Athens. But the translation of these precious documents by "Cornelius" (Guido takes him to be the grandson—*nepos*—of Sallust) is itself unsatisfactory since it unduly abbreviates the originals. Guido therefore returns to the original texts, presumably Greek and Phoenician, to supply the missing information.[25]

The chroniclers of the deeds of the Carolingian heroes and of Arthur's knights follow the same trace. The standard authority for the former is Charlemagne's Archbishop Turpin. This Turpin, or whoever writes in his name, is worthy of belief for he learned of the tragedy of Roncevalles and of Roland's death from a flight of hideous warriors carrying the Saracen Marsirius to hell.[26] The compilers of the chansons de geste regularly cite Turpin as source, though they deviate widely or invent out of whole cloth. As for Arthurian story, Geoffrey of Monmouth asserts that his *History of the Kings of Britain* renders into unadorned Latin the text of "a certain most ancient book in the British language" which was brought to him by Walter, Archdeacon of Oxford, a man expert in "exotic" histories.[27] Wolfram von Eschenbach's *Parzival* is based on Chrétien's grail story, but the child denies his father: "If Master Chrétien de Troyes did not do justice to this story, that may well irk Kyot, who furnished us the right story." This Kyot, says Wolfram, was a Provençal who discovered the original of the Grail story in Toledo, "discarded, set down in

25. Guido de Columnis, *Historia destructionis Troiae*, ed. N. E. Griffin (Cambridge, Mass., Medieval Academy of America, 1936), pp. 3–5.
26. *The Pseudo-Turpin*, ed. H. M. Smyser (Cambridge, Mass., Medieval Academy of America, 1937), p. 87.
27. *The Historia Regum Britanniae of Geoffrey of Monmouth*, ed. A. Griscom (London, Longmans Green, 1929), p. 219.

heathen writing." It had been compiled by a most learned scholar named Flegetanis, a descendant of Solomon. Kyot learned the language in which the book was written and so was able to provide the matter for Wolfram's tale.[28]

The endemic character of this hocus-pocus of documentation needs explanation. Every age produces some more or less successful frauds: the Rowley poems, a Piltdown man, a Protocol of the Elders of Zion. The counterfeiters are intellectually or morally culpable; they cheat in order to create a sensation, for monetary profit, for political ends. But so many writers of so many saints' lives cannot all have been scoundrels.

The explanation is sometimes put forward that medieval authors had no sense of their own importance, that conventionally or not they tried to efface themselves, to deny that they had accomplished anything. Certainly the pose of humility is a very common one. The author undertakes the task because his benefactor has asked him to do so, but it is beyond his powers and he trembles to think about it. He is quite incapable of adding anything of his own. The work is full of flaws which a generous audience is urged to correct. At the same time, he is often careful enough to attach his name to his work, either in a dedication or preface or, more securely, in the text itself, implanted in the rhyme or the body of the prose. Those who, like Chrétien and Chaucer, include a list of their former writings in the text of a new one can scarcely be thought of as desperate for anonymity. Certainly, the twelfth-century Walter Map was not. He had composed an epistle with the title "The Advice of Valerius to Ruffinus the Philosopher Not to Marry." Walter is upset because some people have taken the title seriously and denied his authorship. "My only fault is that I am alive. I have no intention, however, of

28. Wolfram von Eschenbach, *Parzival,* IX.453; XVI.827, tr. Helen M. Mustard and C. E. Passage (New York, Vintage Books, 1961).

correcting this fault by my death. In the title I have changed our names to the names of dead men, for I knew that this giveth pleasure. Otherwise men would have rejected it, as they have me."[29]

Nor can the practice of false documentation be ascribed to medieval reverence for authority. In fact, it argues quite the reverse, for a writer who truly revered his authority would follow him closely. If he merely fleshed out his original by the invention of speeches, descriptions, and moral or philosophical comments he might be understood as exercising a freedom anciently permitted historians. But that freedom scarcely licensed the invention of characters and whole episodes and the alteration of the course of the story.

Again, it is not doubt true that the medieval author had a view of history different from our own. Since the past was valued primarily for what might be learned from it, for the examples of good and evil that it presented, little importance could attach to historical fact, apart, that is, from Biblical narrative. Yet if the truth of the past could be safely ignored, as apparently it was in imaginative literature of classical times, there would be no reason for the usual insistence that the fabricated tale was not fabricated at all.

There is, in fact, no easy explanation for this strange medieval practice. Perhaps it can best be understood as an accommodation of two conflicting attitudes: on the one hand, the insistence of the Judaeo-Christian tradition on veritable report, testified to as by witnesses in a courtroom; on the other, a sense that in tales of the past truth mattered little in comparison with edification or even entertainment. It must be concluded, I think, that the accepted decencies forbade an author, not to make up stories, but to admit that he had. People, evidently, were delighted by stories and rewarded those who told

29. Walter Map, *De nugis curialium,* tr. F. Tupper, and M. B. Ogle (London, Chatto and Windus, 1924), p. 197.

them well. But there was no legitimate category of literature into which the verisimilar fiction could fit. The latitude granted by Lactantius and St. Augustine extended only to rhetorical significations of truth, not to invented tales which might be mistaken for truth, and Boccaccio's defense of "poetry" in Books XIV and XV of *The Genealogy of the Gods* claimed no wider realm, except, perhaps, for the writers of comedy.[30] Perhaps that is why medieval treatises on poetics paid so little attention to invention, the prime division of the discipline of rhetoric in the classical tradition. After all, if the matter of discourse was what happened in the past, or what was said to have happened, the author's subject was given and he had no need to discover what to say. The imagination itself was distrusted as the faculty which distorted and falsified reality.[31] Yet medieval Christianity recognized that while Truth itself must be reserved to the articles of faith, a great body of narrative which might or might not be true was harmless or even salutary. It could not be very wrong, therefore, to pretend to write history, particularly if some good purpose might be alleged for it. The compiler of a manual for preachers remarks of the exemplary tale: "Whether it is the truth of history or fiction doesn't matter because the example is not supplied for its own sake, but for its signification."[32]

If some people were taken in by historical pretense, others must have seen through it and responded either with indignation or with amusement. Only fools could have believed that

30. *Boccaccio on Poetry; Being the Preface and the Fourteenth and Fifteenth Books of Boccaccio's 'Genealogia deorum gentilium,'* tr. Charles G. Osgood (Princeton, N.J., Princeton University Press, 1930), pp. 48–49.

31. See Murray W. Bundy, *The Theory of Imagination in Classical and Medieval Thought,* University of Illinois Studies in Language and Literature. No. 12 (Urbana, Illinois, 1927).

32. Quoted from Bromyard's *Summa predicantium* (c.1390) by G. R. Owst, *Literature and Pulpit in Medieval England,* 2nd ed. (New York, Barnes and Noble, 1961), p. 155. For a perceptive discussion of this attitude, see C. S. Lewis, *The Discarded Image* (Cambridge, Eng., Cambridge University Press, 1964), pp. 179ff.

all of those meticulously documented tales were true history, and if the Middle Ages was in some respects more credulous than our own time it had its share of skeptics. Many accepted Geoffrey of Monmouth's account of the kings of Britain, but his near contemporary, William of Newburgh, denounced it as an outrageous lie. Another writer of the time, Gerald of Wales, made a joke of the matter. He told of a Welshman tormented by evil spirits who was cured when the *Gospel of St. John* was laid on his bosom. But when Geoffrey's history was substituted for the *Gospel* the devils returned in even greater numbers than before.

Perhaps Geoffrey himself intended his story of the Archdeacon Walter's exotic book as a joke, to be recognized as such by the sophisticated in his audience, just as his contemporary Walter Map had hoped that readers would recognize his authorship of the epistle he ascribed to Valerius. It is hard to know. Nothing can be more risky than the attempt to distinguish jest from earnest in the literature of the distant past for we are aliens to the culture and insensitive to its nuances. If Geoffrey was joking, he was saying to those of his readers who understood him that his work was neither history nor pretended history, not a fraud but his own invention, a work of fiction.

Wolfram von Eschenbach's story of Flegetanis seems so farfetched that I am inclined to take it as such a joke. Is Chrétien serious when he ends his tale of Yvain. "I never heard any more told of it, nor will you ever hear any further particulars unless some one wishes to add some lies"? When Boccaccio asserts of his *Teseide*, "I wish to write in rhyme an ancient story, so hidden in time that no Latin author tells it," one is tempted to ask what language he read it in. He may speak sober truth when he claims that for his *Genealogy of the Gods* he relied heavily upon a treatise by one "Theodontius" in the collection of a friend, Paul of Perugia, but that "to the very serious inconvenience of this book of mine, I found that his saucy wife Biella, after his death, wilfully destroyed this and many other books of Paul's."[33] But we are secure in recognizing the quality of his defense of the historical truth of the tales of the *Decameron:* "As for those who say that these matters fell out otherwise than as I relate them, I should account it no small favour, if they would produce the originals, and should what I write not accord with them, I would acknowledge the justice of their censure, and study to amend my ways."[34]

Surely there were members of the court of Richard II who doubted the existence of that account of the Trojan war by Lollius from which Chaucer claimed he drew the matter of his *Troilus*, perhaps others who recognized the dependence of the poem on Boccaccio's *Filostrato*. If so, we must suppose that the attribution to Lollius was jocular and was so understood by the audience or by that part of it to which the poet primarily addressed himself. That this is the case is made evident, I believe, by Chaucer's hiding behind his mysterious "author" whenever the tale demands that he say something derogatory about the fair Criseyde. The effect is not unlike that of his insistence in the *Canterbury Tales* that he is merely an honest reporter and therefore not responsible for the nasty tales other people tell. Whether or not "Lollius" is a joke, no shadow of doubt can attach to Chaucer's comment on his tale of a rooster and a hen:

> This storie is also trewe, I undertake,
> As is the book of Launcelot de Lake,
> That wommen holde in ful great reverence[35]

33. *Boccaccio on Poetry*, p. 114. A. Hortis, *Studi sulle opere latine del Boccaccio* (Trieste, 1879), pp. 464–468, and Carlo Landi, *Demogorgone* (Palermo, Sandron, 1930), pp. 18–20, argue that there was indeed a Theodontius or Theodotius who wrote about Troy, perhaps in the ninth century. Whether there was or not, the case for Boccaccio's dependence upon him is no stronger than that for Chaucer's reliance upon Lollius.

34. Boccaccio, *Decameron*, Prologue to the Fourth Day, tr. J. M. Rigg.

35. Nun's Priest's Tale, in Chaucer's *Canterbury Tales*, ll. 3211–3.

When a story is understood to be fiction, the witness who vouches for its historical truth becomes part of the fiction himself. He is no longer outside the story, giving testimony; he is inside and plays a part himself. As fictional narrator, he colors the story in terms of his own nature, so giving it a quality deliberately different from objective reporting. Renaissance fiction exploits this device in a variety of ways.

Sometimes the citation of source, like the work itself, becomes a burlesque of medieval narrative and the credulous oafs who read it and believed it. In the tradition of the chansons de geste Ariosto calls upon Archbishop Turpin to testify to the truth of the adventures of Orlando and Ruggiero. The poet rises to defend the veracity of his story against the objection that the island where six mounted knights were said to have fought in bitter battle was in fact so mountainous and rocky that there was on it no foot of even ground. The apparent discrepancy, Ariosto hastens to explain, was the result of an earthquake which had occurred since the time of the battle, and he begs his critic to clear his reputation of the accusation of lying.[36] We are told, surely not in all seriousness, that the record of the deeds of Esplandian, son of Amadis, was brought to Spain by a Hungarian merchant who had found it by chance in a hermitage near Constantinople, buried under a tomb of stone, the writing and the parchment so ancient that it could be read only with the greatest difficulty.[37] The chronicle of Gargantua was found by Jean Audeau in a tomb under a meadow near Narsay: "a big, fat, great, grey, pretty, small, mouldy, little pamphlet, smelling stronger, but no better than roses. In that book the said genealogy was found written all at length, in a chancery hand, not in paper, not in parchment, nor in wax, but in the bark of an elm-tree, yet so worn with

36. Ariosto, *Orlando Furioso,* Canto XLII, stanzas 20–22.
37. Prologue of the Spanish author, in *Le Premier Livre de Amadis de Gaulle,* tr. Seigneur des Essars, Nicolas de Herberay (Paris, 1548), Sig. Av^r.

the long tract of time, that hardly could three letters together be there perfectly discerned."[38]

The joke is more intricate in More's *Utopia*. The book is a traveler's tale, More tells us, one which has to do with an even greater marvel than Scyllas and greedy Harpies and folk-devouring Laestrygonians, that is, with that human improbability, a community of well and wisely trained citizens. More is much upset when he hears that "an unusually sharp person" has doubts about the truth of his story. If he had intended to write a fiction, he points out, he would have provided some indications for the learned sort to see through to his purpose. He would therefore have invented meaningful names instead of those barbarous, meaningless ones that his faith as a historian required him to use: Utopia, Anydrus, and the like.[39] Of course, More's learned readers knew that those Greek-derived names meant No Place, River Without Water, and so on. The satire, then, is on the fools of More's own day, those who know no Greek, have no understanding of literature, and cannot tell jest from earnest or fiction from history.

Sancho Panza says of his story about the shepherdess Torralva, "He that told me the tale said it was so certain and true, that I might, when I told it to any other, very well swear and affirm that I had seen it all myself."[40] And Cid Hamet Benengeli, chronicler of the famous history of Don Quixote, begins a chapter with these words, "I swear like a Catholic Christian" —on which his "translator" Cervantes comments that though Cid Hamet was a Moor, "as the Catholic Christian, when he

38. Rabelais, *Gargantua and Pantagruel*, Bk. I, ch. 1, tr. T. Urquhart and P. A. Motteux.

39. Letter to Peter Giles, in *The Complete Works of St. Thomas More*, Vol. IV, *Utopia*, ed. Edward Surtz, S.J., and J. H. Hexter (New Haven, Conn., Yale University Press, 1965), pp. 248ff.

40. Cervantes, *Don Quixote*, I.20, tr. Thomas Shelton. On this subject, see Bruce Wardropper, " 'Don Quixote': Story or History?" *Modern Philology*, LXIII (1965), 1–11.

swears, doth or ought to swear truth, so did he as if he had sworn like a Catholic Christian in what he meant to write of Don Quixote."[41] But Cervantes' play with the question of truth and fiction goes beyond such jesting. The world in which the mad Don moves is no fantasy like the worlds of Orlando, Gargantua, Hythloday, and the Red Cross Knight. It is very like the truth, rather ugly and harsh. Within this verisimilar fiction there are the extravagant tales which Don Quixote takes to be sober history, tales about impossibly heroic knights, impossibly beautiful women, impossibly evil magicians. The verisimilar fiction and the absurd history confront each other when the Canon urges Don Quixote to come to his senses, to recognize the distinction between the true and the false. By the end of their colloquy we are no longer sure that there is such a distinction.

Despite the mockery of such sophisticated uses the practice of false documentation does not die out, as the prefaces of Aphra Behn, Defoe, Richardson, and countless others amply testify. Yet some storytellers, or perhaps the tellers of some kinds of story, become willing to admit that their tales may not be true. A century or so after Chaucer wrote *Troilus and Criseyde* the Scottish poet Henryson takes up the subject again. He pretends to be doubtful of the account that Chaucer derived from Lollius: "Quha wait gif all that Chauceir wrait was trew?" As for his own version, he claims only the vaguest of authorities, "ane uther quair," and he will not guarantee the truth of this book, either:

> Nor I wait nocht gif this narratioun
> Be authoreist, or fenyeit of the new
> Be sum Poeit, throw his Inventioun[42]

41. Cervantes, *Don Quixote,* II.27.
42. Robert Henryson, *The Poems and Fables,* ed. H. Harvey Wood, 2nd ed. (Edinburgh, Oliver and Boyd, 1958), p. 107.

The conventional effort to convince the reader that the story is history has here disappeared; all that remains is the conventional effort to shoulder some "uther quair" with the responsibility. In other writers the prefatory declaration weakens into what is in effect a confession that the tale is fiction, often accompanied by a formula like that used to justify apocryphal testaments. Caxton is dubious about *Mort d'Arthur:* "And for to passe the tyme thys book shal be plesaunte to rede in, but for to gyve fayth and beleve that al is trewe that is conteyned herein, ye be at your liberte."[43] Bonaventure des Périers assures the readers of his collection of novellas: "Il ne faut point plorer de tout cecy que je vous compte, car peultestre qu'il n'est pas vray." And again, "Je ne sçay pas si vous m'en croyez, mais il n'est pas damné qui ne le croit."[44] The French version of *Amadis* is justified for the reader by its translator, Nicolas de Herberay, not as a true story, for it is derived from no famous author, but "pour le passetemps & plaisir qu'il pourra recevoir en la bienvoyant."[45] The Elizabethan translator of the history of Eusebius advises his audience: "If you happen to light upon any story that savoureth of superstition, or that seemeth impossible, refer it to the Author, take it as cheap as ye finde it, remember that the holy Ghost saith, *omnis homo mendax:* If so, peradventure the Reader too, then let the one bear with the other."[46] And toward the end of the sixteenth century an English storyteller says plainly

43. *The Prologues and Epilogues of William Caxton,* ed. W. J. B. Crotch, Early English Text Society, O.S. 176 (London, Oxford University Press, 1928), p. 95.

44. Cited from Tales, nos. 66, 67, by Krystyna Kasprzyk, *Nicolas de Troyes et le Genre Narratif en France au XVIe Siècle* (Warsaw, Państwowe Wydawnictwo Naukowe, 1963), p. 328.

45. *Le Premier Livre de Amadis,* dedication to Charles, Duc d'Orleans.

46. Eusebius, *The Ecclesiastical History,* tr. Meredith Hanmer (London, 1650 [first printed, 1584]), Sig. A4r.

that his tales "are but forged onely for delight, neither credible to be believed nor hurtfull to be perused."[47]

The open admission that a story is "forged" reflects a growing recognition that history and fiction are distinct kinds of literature. The difference between tales that are told "for true" and tales that are not, between history and story, *histoire* and *histoire, geschichte* and *geschichte,* was not ignored in the Middle Ages; the same kind of belief was surely not accorded Froissart's *Chronicle* and *Troilus and Criseyde.* But knowledge of the past was itself subordinated to other values and in any case could not be relied upon. The unquestionable verity of Biblical story relegated all other histories to the realm of human uncertainty,[48] so that a very large body of apocryphal, hagiological, and quasi-historical narrative, if not demonstrably false or harmful to the soul, could be tolerated as perhaps true.

Even as late as the sixteenth century, Antonio de Guevara thought he could justify his fabrication of the *Libro del Emperador Marco Aurelio* on such grounds. He had claimed that the work was a translation of a volume found in the library of Cosimo de Medici. A learned "bachelor," Pedro de Rhua (or Rua), detected the fraud and addressed two letters to Guevara remarking on the inconsistencies and anachronisms in the book and on its conflicts with the classical historians. Guevara replied by pointing out that authorities in the realm of humanities differed so from one another that "apart from divine writings, it is not necessary either to affirm or to deny any of them." In fact, he continues, "I regard very few of them as other than a source of amusement . . . Do not, Sir, dwell upon

47. Barnaby Rich, *His Farewell to Militarie Profession* (1581), in *Eight Novels* (London, for the Shakespeare Society, 1846), p. 16.
48. For the persistence of the attitude which regarded the Bible as the only infallible history, see Herschel Baker, *The Race of Time* (Toronto, University of Toronto Press, 1967), pp. 35ff.

pagan and secular histories, for none is more reliable than another, *et pro utraque parte militant argumenta.*"[49]

To this defense, Rhua responds in a third letter by identifying Guevara's position with that of the skeptics Pyrrho, Arcesilaüs, and Lacydes. Such skepticism, he exclaims, denies the possibility of human knowledge, of rational guidance, of communication between the past and the present, the present and the future. He grants the legitimacy of tales represented as fictions by their authors. But to relegate all secular history to the realm of fiction is to take the sun out of the world, as the Athenian philosopher Athenagoras says. To be sure, some historians are less reliable than others—the ancient Greeks are particularly untrustworthy since they valued style and eloquence above the truth—but the consensus of the learned can distinguish between those who are worthy of belief and those who are not.

By the sixteenth century the idea was gaining currency

---

49. The Rhua-Guevara correspondence is printed in *Biblioteca de Autores Españoles, desde la formacion del lenguaje hasta nuestra dias. Epistolario Español,* ed. Don Eugenio de Ochoa (Madrid, 1850), I, 229–250. Guevara's letter is dated 9 August (1540): "Muy virtuoso Señor: Es verdad que hogaño rescibi otra letra de Vm., y téngole en merced aquella y esta, que suplen lo poco que yo sé y lo mucho en que yerro. Son muy pocas las cosas que ha notado en mis obrillas, y serán sus avisos para remirar lo hecho y emendar lo venidero. Como, señor, sabeis, son tan varios los escriptores en esta arte de humanidad, que, fuera de las letras divinas, no hay qué afirmar ni qué negar en ninguna dellas; y para decir la verdad, a muy pocas dellas creo mas de tomar en ellas un pasatiempo. ¿Y á qué se ha de dar fe? pues hay doctores, y aun Sabellico quiere sentir, que fué burla lo de Troya, sino que los griegos fuéron destruidos. ¿Y qué dirá que otros dicen que el verdadero Hércules fué Sanson? A cuya opinion se llega el Testado. No haga Vm. hincapié en historias gentiles y profanas, pues no tenemos mas certinidad que digan verdad unos que otros, *et pro utraque parte militant argumenta.* Y en lo demas yo huelgo de saber de sa salud, y que esté bueno; y ansi haré por acá todo lo que le cumpliere. De Valladolid á 9 de agosto. A servicio de Vm."

that something approaching certitude about what had happened in the past was not unattainable and, more important, was worth striving for. That a change from the medieval attitude occurs during the Renaissance is made evident by the appearance of a lively and prolonged discussion concerning the nature of imaginative literature, much of it devoted to defining the difference between fiction and history and to weighing their respective virtues. There were now more clearly than before two kinds of story (the Bible apart) rather than varieties of one.

ii

THE DIFFERENCE BETWEEN FICTION AND HISTORY

Recognition that story belongs to a category different from history implies the demarcation of a line between them. That line is not easy to draw, and the problem continues to occupy the attention of modern critics and philosophers.[1] The apparently simple distinction between truth and falsehood proves difficult to apply even to the narrative genres. Histories "never can be true," according to the *Mirror for Magistrates*, because of "affection, fere, or doubtes that dayly brue."[2] Since even the most scrupulous historian must select, organize, and conjecture, he cannot produce an account which truly represents what happened in the past. The inventor of story, on the other side, is unable to dispense with fact, for his most fantastic fiction must necessarily incorporate correspondences with human experience.

In practice, modern librarians and booksellers rarely find it difficult to separate "fiction" from "nonfiction." (Oddly, the category of "fiction" now seems to exclude "poetry," once almost

1. See, for example, R. G. Collingwood, *The Idea of History* (Oxford, Clarendon Press, 1946), pp. 245ff.; Frank Kermode, "Novel, History and Type," in *Novel*, I (1967–68), 231–238; and Warner Berthoff, "Fiction, History, Myth: Notes toward the Discrimination of Narrative Forms," *Harvard English Studies*, I (1970), 263–287. As this book goes to press, the *London Times Literary Supplement* of March 23, 1973 (No. 3, 707, pp. 315–316 and 327–328) publishes essays by Mary Renault and A. J. P. Taylor entitled respectively "History in Fiction" and "Fiction in History."

2. *Mirror for Magistrates*, ed. L. B. Campbell (Cambridge, Eng., Cambridge University Press, 1938), p. 198.

synonymous with it.) But the signs by which they make this distinction became current only after the novel had developed into a conventional form. Before that time, there lay between the obviously historical narrative and the obviously invented one a region in which the reader had no sure guide. Of course, as Sidney says, no one but a fool would mistake a beast fable for the truth. Other kinds of narrative came safely within the province of fiction because they were incredible and therefore could not be history, or because their literary form conventionally licensed departure from it: tales of pagan gods and heroes, dream visions, moral allegories, dialogues, and comedies. Narratives written in verse seemed more likely to be fictional than those written in prose because of the artificiality of the medium and because poetry was traditionally the father of lies. Histories were supposed to follow chronological order; not so fictions, or rather those that obeyed Horace's prescriptions for the heroic poem. Despite such clues, there remained a great many ambiguous cases. Most writers of the Renaissance described Xenophon's *Cyropedia* as fictional, but Jacques de Vintemille who made a French version of it insisted that Xenophon was as true a historian as Livy, Plutarch, and Thucydides.[3] Although *Amadis* was usually thought of as a delightful fiction, an English translator saw fit to introduce it with reference to Cicero's praise of histories and to dilate on the advantage of learning from the lessons of the past.[4] How was the reader to know whether Bandello's story of Romeo and Juliet and Gascoigne's *Adventures of Master F. I.* were fact or fancy? Or a much later instance, Defoe's *Journal of the Plague Year*? Were the tragedies of Richard, Duke of York, and of King Lear equally "true chronicle history"?

For the purpose of differentiating between fiction and his-

3. Xenophon, *La Cyropedie,* tr. Jacques de Vintemille (Paris, 1547).

4. A. M., dedicatory epistle to *The Third Booke of Amadis de Gaule* (London, 1618), addressed to Sir Philip Herbert.

tory Renaissance discussions limited the latter as truth to *res
gestae,* unadorned reporting of things that had happened, free
of distortion, addition, or omission, as though it were possible
to record human actions in words as faithfully as a musical
performance might be recorded by an infallible phonograph.
History so understood excluded not only the classical liberty
of inventing speeches and battle descriptions but also accounts of ancient actions for which testimony was dubious
and even artistic composition. To be sure, bare reporting of
ascertainable fact was not the kind of historiography that the
humanists learned from their classical models. Intelligent historians considered it their duty to make judgments and to
speculate as to why things happened as well as to record what
had happened. Camden quotes Polybius approvingly: "Take
away from History Why, How, and To what end, things have
been done, and Whether the thing done hath succeeded according to Reason; and all that remains will rather be an idle
Sport and Foolery, than a profitable Instruction."[5] Despite such
reservations, the simplistic conception of history as "the declaration of true things in order set foorth" (so Thomas Cooper's
Thesaurus defines *historia*) was often asserted as the ideal to
be striven for. Jacques Amyot introduces his translation of
Plutarch with the assertion that, in contrast to poetry, history
deals only with "la nue verité."[6] "Hystoriographers ought not
to fayne anye Orations nor any other thing, but truely to re-
porte every such speach, and deede, even as it was spoken or
done," declares Thomas Blundeville in *The true order and
Methode of wryting and reading Hystories.*[7] Edmond Howes

5. William Camden, *The History of the Most Renowned and
Victorious Princess Elizabeth, Selected Chapters,* ed. W. T. Mac-
Caffrey (Chicago, University of Chicago Press, 1970), p. 6.
   6. Jacques Amyot, "Aux lecteurs" (1559), in Bernard Weinberg,
Critical Prefaces of the French Renaissance (Evanston, Ill., Northwestern University Press, 1950), p. 167.
   7. Thomas Blundeville, *The true order and Methode of wryting
and reading Hystories* (London, 1574), Sig. E iv.

warns his reader to expect no filed phrases, ink-horn terms, uncouth words, nor fantastic speeches but good plain English, "rightly befitting Chronologie."[8] It is this conception of history as reporting unsullied by the falseness of art to which Thomas More jocularly alludes in apologizing to his friend Peter Giles for his delay in completing *Utopia*. The delay is really inexcusable, he says, for he had no need to invent his material or to arrange it. "I had only to repeat what in your company I heard Raphael relate. Hence there was no reason for me to take trouble about the style of the narrative."[9]

An idea of history that denied the classical license to invent speeches and descriptions, that rendered improper the retailing of improbable traditions, however venerable, and rejected artistic composition because it detracted from the impression of naked truthfulness tended to separate the discipline of the historian from that of the poet. The division was made sharper by a growing concern of historians for the authenticity of their sources, a characteristic of what has been called the "historical revolution" and the "reaction against humanism" which took place toward the end of the sixteenth century and the beginning of the seventeenth.[10] William Camden abandons the liberties of the ancient historians: "Speeches and Orations, unless they be the very same *verbatim*, or else abbreviated, I have

8. Address to "the honest and understanding reader" in Edmond Howes, *The Annales or Generall Chronicle of England, Begun First by Maister John Stow* (London, 1615).

9. *The Complete Works of St. Thomas More*, Vol. IV, *Utopia*, ed. Edward Surtz, S.J., and J. H. Hexter (New Haven, Conn., Yale University Press, 1965), p. 39.

10. See F. S. Fussner, *The Historical Revolution, English Historical Writing and Thought 1580–1640* (New York, Columbia University Press, 1962). Eduard Fueter, *Geschichte der neueren Historiographie* (Munich, Oldenbourg, 1936; reprinted, New York, 1968), pp. 307ff., describes the movement as "Die Reaktion gegen das Humanismus" which he dates "Um die Wende des 16. Jahrhunderts."

not medled withall, much less coined them of mine own Head."[11] Although Livy began his history of Rome with an account of Romulus and Remus, Samuel Daniel begins his *Collections of the Historie of England* not with Trojan Brutus but with William the Conqueror because "it was but our curiosity to search further backe into times past than we might discerne."[12] The new attitude toward historiography was clearly manifested in the undertaking by the Bollandist fathers of the great task of seeking out the earliest texts of the saints' lives and freeing them from the accretions and decorations of the Middle Ages. The humanist-trained predecessors of the Bollandists had understood hagiography as an art with a moral purpose. They described the medieval legends as "praevaricata atque falsa," but it was the rudeness of style to which they referred, not the historical account. Matters could be set right by using proper locutions, omitting irrelevances and absurdities, adding what was necessary for completeness and coherence, and setting all in proper order. When the Jesuit Father Héribert Roswey (or Rosweyde), John Bollandus, and their successors undertook to compile a legendary not as a stylistic revision but rather in opposition to it, on the basis of the oldest available manuscripts, they reflected the new trend in historical attitudes. They rather frightened the sainted Cardinal Bellarmine. In a letter dated from Rome in 1608 he expressed grave doubts about the project. What good would it lead to, he asked. Was it not probable that recourse to the original stories would reveal much that was inept, childish, and absurd, more likely to produce laughter than edification? Despite these objections, the work went forward; historical method supplanted

11. Camden, *History of Princess Elizabeth*, p. 6.
12. Samuel Daniel, *The Collection of the History of England* (London, 1634), Sig. B i[r]. Despite this assertion, Daniel does devote a few prefatory pages to the history of Britain before the Conquest. Of Arthur he says that he was "worthy to have been a subject of truth to posterity, and not of fiction (as Legendary Writers have made him)." Sig. B 4[v].

revision for style, verisimilitude, and moral effect.[13]

Not all historians were ready to abandon the quasi-historical realm and to restrict themselves to the evidence of reliable sources. Sir Walter Ralegh, for example, claimed the privilege of supplying "conjectures" to fill the lacunae of history, with the proviso that what was supplied should not be subject to disproof. He tells a story to make his point. He had taken prisoner Don Pedro de Sarmiento, a worthy Spanish gentleman. Ralegh was curious about a map of the Straits of Magellan that the Spaniard had with him. "When I asked him . . . some question about an Island in those Streights, which methought, might have done either benefit or displeasure to his enterprise, he told me merrily that it was to be called the *Painters Wives Island;* saying That whilst the Fellow drew that Map, his Wife sitting by, desired him to put in one Country for her; that she, in imagination, might have an Island of her own." In an age of exploration, of course, painters' wives' islands located by latitude and longitude must inevitably be found out. "But," Ralegh observes, "in filling up the Blanks of old Histories we need not be so scrupulous. For it is not to be feared, that time should run backward, and by restoring the things themselves to knowledge, make our conjectures appear ridiculous."[14]

As historians were beginning to withdraw from such freedoms, Renaissance storytellers and their apologists seized upon them as their proper realm. That which was neither true nor demonstrably a lie, the long ago and—despite Ralegh— the far away about which historians and geographers had no reliable information, came to be accepted as the appropriate domain for fictional invention. Ronsard is explicit: "Tu noteras encores, Lecteur, ce poinct qui te menera tout droict au

13. Hippolyte Delehaye, S.J., *L'Oeuvre des Bollandistes à travers trois siècles,* 2nd. ed. (Brussels, Société des Bollandistes, 1959), pp. 14ff.
14. Walter Ralegh, *The History of the World,* Pt. I, Bk. 2, ch. xxiii, sec. 4, quoted from the edition of London, 1687.

vray chemin des Muses: c'est que le Poete ne doit jamais prendre l'argument de son oeuvre, que trois ou quatre cens ans ne soient passez pour le moins, afin que personne ne vive plus de son temps, qui le puisse de ses fictions & vrayes semblances convaincre . . ." Even the great antiquity of a story might on occasion prove an insufficient defense, for Vergil, Ronsard points out, erred in lying "contre la verité de la chose" when he made Dido and Aeneas contemporaries for in fact she antedated him by at least a century.[15] Vauquelin de la Fresnaye gives similar instruction to the poet:

> pour n'estre dedit, il faut bien advertir
> De prendre un argument ou l'on puisse mentir.[16]

The Spaniard López Pinciano answers a query as to why Heliodorus lacks a basis in history: "In this as in all the rest Heliodorus was most prudent, for he used kings of unknown lands in his argument and their truth and falsehood can be ill ascertained."[17] Mazzoni allows poets "to depart from the truth in all those things of which the people for whose benefit the poem is written has no firm and sure knowledge. But when the events have happened in the present time and in the country of the people in whose language the poem is written, then the poet cannot depart from the truth, for he would openly be held a liar."[18] Tasso similarly warns against subjects drawn

15. Pierre de Ronsard, *Préface sur 'La Franciade'* (1587) in *Oeuvres complètes,* ed. Paul Laumonier (Paris, Hachette, 19;i0), XVI, 345.

16. Vauquelin de la Fresnaye, *L'Art Poètique,* 1, 909–910, ed. Georges Pellisier (Paris, 1885).

17. López Pinciano, *Philosophia antiqua poetica,* ed. Alfredo Carballo Picazo (Madrid, Instituto "Miguel Cervantes," 1953), II, 195 (Epistola undecima).

18. Quoted by Bernard Weinberg, *A History of Literary Criticism in the Italian Renaissance* (Chicago, University of Chicago Press, 1961), II, 644, from Mazzoni, *Della difesa della Comedia di Dante* (1688, first printed 1587), p. 63.

from nearby lands, but "among distant peoples and in unknown countries we can easily feign many things without taking away the authority from the story. Therefore from the land of Goths and from Norway and Sweden and Iceland or from the East Indies or the countries recently discovered in the vast ocean beyond the pillars of Hercules, the subjects of such poems should be taken."[19]

This recognition of an area in which fictional invention might have freedom received even diplomatic confirmation. In 1522, Juan Luis Vives, Spanish humanist and educator, published a dialogue entitled "Truth Dressed Up, or of Poetic License: To What Extent Poets May Be Permitted to Vary from the Truth."[20] Vives' friend Vergara tells him of the appearance of Truth and her train at an entrance to the house of mankind. She is not theological truth, that truth concerning which Pilate asked Christ but did not stay for the answer. Rather, she is truth as it is commonly understood, the "truth" that is heard about so often in the marketplace and seen so rarely. She is dressed plainly, like a rustic, wears a severe expression, and is accompanied by her husband Fear and her son Hate. At the other portal appears False with his cohorts, false in everything, no doubt a hermaphrodite, of urban or rather courtly elegance, richly dressed, bejeweled, bedaubed with cosmetics. Truth sends Plato and other great men to urge

19. Torquato Tasso, *Del Poema eroico*, II, tr. A. Gilbert, *Literary Criticism: Plato to Dryden* (New York, American Book Company, 1940), p. 488. See also Paolo Beni, *Comparazione di Omero, Virgilio, e Torquato* in *Opere di Torquato Tasso* (Pisa, 1828), XXI, 218–219.

20. J. L. Vives, "Veritas fucata, sive de licentia poetica, quantum Poëtis liceat a Veritate abscedere," *Opera omnia* (Valencia, 1782), II, 517–531. According to the editor's note the dialogue was published at Louvain in 1522 by Theodoric Martin. It should not be confused with a tract bearing a similar title "Ioannis Lodovici Vivis Valentini in suum Christi triumphum Praelectio quae dicitur Veritas fucata." The latter was published in *Joannis Lodovici Vives Opuscula varia* (Louvain, Theodoric Martin, 1519), sigs. s ii^r-t i^r.

the adherents of False to desert him, but the appeal is derided since Truth, though she may be a queen, possesses not even a gold bracelet. But after the failure of this mission a strong feeling develops in the camp of False that Truth must be acknowledged as the proper mistress of human minds and that therefore an attempt should be made to arrive at a treaty between the opposing parties. Any such treaty, however, must provide that Truth submit herself to the rule of False since men of refined ears and education cannot tolerate her harsh and rude manner. A legation consisting of Homer, Hesiod, Lucian, and Apuleius presents the proposal to Truth, arguing that rare and admirable garments would enhance her authority and the veneration due her. Although Truth protests that she would prefer to go naked she reluctantly responds with a compromise draft of ten articles, the substance of which follows:

1. Those who are called "poets" in Greek (*auctores, sive compositores, sive fictores*) may relate whatever distortions and embellishments of Truth that Public Fame (that monster of many heads) has concocted. But he who makes up the whole of what he tells is to be thought a fool, or rather a liar, than a poet.[21]

2. The historically confused period before the institution of the Olympic games (that is, four hundred years after the destruction of Troy and thirty years before the foundation of Rome) is a field free for embellishment, as long as a nucleus of truth is retained. Later writers, however, may not alter what was written by great poets of ancient times and accepted by public opinion.

---

21. "Nam confingere aliquem eorum, et comminisci id totum quod referat, ineptum videbitur, et mendacem potius, quàm poëtam esse." Compare Lactantius, *Institutes*, I.11: "Totum autem, quod referas, fingere, id est ineptum esse, et mendacem potius, quam poëtam."

3. To Truth is reserved whatever occurred after the first Olympiad, save that some embellishment may be permitted to give the story beauty, pleasure, or public utility. Such poetic practices, however, should not impair the truth of the work.

4. A mixture of truth and invention may be permitted in the relation of things that happened before the Olympic games which are known to be fabulous and are presented as such.

5. Since latitude should be given to efforts to cultivate morality, writers may invent apologues out of whole cloth. "New" comedies portraying human passions and dialogues which tend to the improvement of manners may also be permitted.

6. Free license is given to the use of many varieties of rhetorical figure for the embellishment of Truth.

7. In the exposition of arts and learning, whether in verse or in prose, no deviation from Truth is permitted save for the use of metaphor.

8. Whatever dressing up may be given to Truth must be characterized by verisimilitude, consistency, and decorum.

9. Any of the train of False who takes no account of morality or utility may be tolerated if he openly professes his nature. He may be allowed Milesian citizenship. He may be accompanied by the two wives of Vulcan (Aglaia and Venus?) and dwell with Lucian, Apuleius, and Clodius Albinus the Roman emperor.[22]

10. Anyone acting contrary to these provisions is to be expelled from the schools and academies without honor, name, money, class, land, or citizenship.

22. Clodius Albinus is described as a friend of Apuleius and author of "Milesian" tales "written in but a mediocre style" by Julius Capitolinus, "Vita Clodii Albini," XI.8 and XII.12, in *Scriptores historiae Augustae,* I, ed. David Magie (Loeb edition).

These clauses are to be inscribed by public scriveners, partly by Terentius Varro, partly by Horace, and partly by Lactantius.

The terms of Truth's treaty fairly present the usual Renaissance position. Freedom to invent whole stories is limited to the genres of allegory and beast fable, dramatic comedy, dialogue, and such tales as Lucian and Apuleius told—Milesian tales, Vives calls them, of the kind that nurses tell children by the fireside to keep them from crying.[23] For the rest, while the author is required to observe, more or less respectfully, whatever is known or generally accepted about the past, the less substantial that knowledge the greater the permissible admixture of invention. The way opens, therefore, for fiction set in the far away or long ago to take the form of history without pretending to be history, to present itself as a work of the imagination. When such stories are documented (as *Utopia* and *Gargantua* are), the documentation becomes an obvious jest.

At the conclusion of his dialogue, Vives expresses doubt that poets, "that tribe of wandering and free men," would complacently accept restriction within the narrow bounds of Truth's treaty. The event proved him right. Outside those bounds lies the world near at hand, the world of *Pamela* and the great succession of "realistic" novels. Critical theorists of the Renaissance did grant to the writer of "new comedy"—the comedy of Menander and Terence—the right to set fictional stories about private people in the contemporary scene, and on precisely the ground that such stories could not be proved false.[24] Although the privilege did not extend to genres other than

23. J. L. Vives, *De ratione dicendi*, III.6, in *Opera omnia*, II, 216.
24. See, for example, Giraldi Cinthio, *Discorsi intorno al comporre de i romanzi, delle commedie, e delle tragedie* (Venice, 1554), p. 208, tr. Gilbert, *Literary Criticism*, p. 253; Lodovico Castelvetro, *Poetica d'Aristotele vulgarizzata et sposta* (Basel, 1576), IX.189, tr. Gilbert, *Literary Criticism*, p. 320; Torquato Tasso, *Discorsi del poema eroico*, II, in *Opere* (Pisa, 1823), XII, 32–33.

comedy, some post-Renaissance authors of nondramatic "domestic" fictions—Sorel, Congreve, and Fielding, for example—nevertheless sought to legitimize their stories by appeal to that ancient license.

The grant of a limited territory to the writer of fiction freed him from the charge of trespassing on truth and therefore of lying, but it rendered more acute the problem of justifying his work. Separation from history set invented story in competition with history as to its value for mankind. The historian's credentials were patent, and they were supported by such impressive testimony as Cicero's endlessly repeated phrase, "History bears witness to the passing of the ages, sheds light upon reality, gives life to recollection and guidance to human existence, and brings tidings of ancient days."[25] It offered the painful lessons of the past for the painless instruction of the present. And above all it was light upon reality, not the mirage of imagination.

The response to this formidable challenge claimed that while history might be true to the particulars of the past, good fiction was truth of another kind. If I may compress the arguments of this weighty, complex, and subtle literature of apology into very brief compass, the Renaissance defenders of poetry followed medieval precedent in proposing that fiction, like ancient myth and Biblical parable, was a rhetorical device for expressing moral, religious, or historical truths, useful because it was delightful and memorable and because the difficulty of extracting its meaning enhanced the value of the meaning as the toughness of the nutshell sweetens the kernel. They added compatible defenses drawn from Plato and Aristotle which asserted that fictional creation represented ideas or universals or human types rather than individuals, imitations philosophically more true than the particularity to which history was bound. Or fiction was taken to show the truth of the world as

25. Cicero, *De oratore*, II.ix.36 (Loeb edition).

it might be and should be, a rational world in which virtue was rewarded and vice punished and therefore a world more "real" than the foolish one of the historians. A central tendency of Renaissance critical theory identified or closely associated fiction (whether in prose or in verse) with "poetry," so that the feigning of the storyteller, his making or creating, was described as his distinctive poetic function, and his tale, like the Homeric poems, the *Cyropedia*, and the *Aeneid*, became instruction for princes and guidance for the commonwealth.

These high claims for the moral value of invented story required the Renaissance apologists to dissociate "poetry" from medieval romance. The tales of the knights of Charlemagne and of Arthur could not easily be justified in terms of their benefit to society. They must have been composed by barbarous and ignorant entertainers (for Protestants, "monkish" ones) and had as little to do with true poetic invention as diseased fantasy with sane imagination. Typically, therefore, verisimilitude was offered as the quality of good fiction that differentiated it from the wild dreams of medieval romancers on the one hand and made it comparable or even superior in value to veritable history on the other. This might be construed as advocacy of "realism," a quality not much in evidence in Renaissance literature. But there was little agreement among Renaissance theorists as to what the Aristotelian term implied, what kind of truth a fiction should be like, and what was meant by its likeness to truth. The word was used variously, as Hathaway and Weinberg have shown.[26] Sometimes it meant merely the avoidance of patent falsehood, absurdity, or inconsistency, sometimes one or another of the varieties of philosophical as opposed to historical truth, sometimes observation of the rule of decorum, sometimes the possible or probable

26. See especially Baxter Hathaway, *Marvels and Commonplaces: Renaissance Literary Criticism* (New York, Random House, 1968), pp. 54ff., and the passages listed in the index to Weinberg's *History of Literary Criticism in the Italian Renaissance, s.v.* "verisimilitude."

in accordance with natural order and with due consideration for cause and effect, sometimes that which common opinion would credit. For some, truth-likeness excluded historical truth; for others it was founded on such truth or approximated it. Since it was probable that improbable things should happen, it was argued that they were therefore verisimilar and fit matter for fiction. Verisimilitude was denied to the *Divine Comedy* on the ground that a living man could not make a voyage through the regions of the other world and because a poet's account of his own actions could not command belief; the truth-likeness of the poem was asserted because the example of the underworld travels of Theseus, Hercules, and St. Paul attested to it and because the absolute power of God justified the action, even if impossible. There were similiar disagreements with regard to the verisimilitude of *Orlando Furioso,* *Gerusalemme Liberata,* and Guarini's *Il Pastor Fido.* So broad was the range of its meanings that it was even construed to accommodate the beast fable, provided the story was given an air of plausibility and the animals spoke and acted in the character that common opinion assigned to them.

Sir Philip Sidney saw no difference in didactic force between verity and the verisimilar. Having urged that the poet's freedom from fact allows him to create instances emotionally more powerful and morally and philosophically superior to historical ones, he asks his reader to compare a real incident reported by Herodotus and Justinian with a similar but invented tale of Xenophon's. Since the stories are equivalent in moral import and no difference is suggested in the manner of their telling, the issue is limited to a comparison of the didactic effectiveness of historical verity and imagined story. Sidney's conclusion is flat: "A feigned example hath as much force to teach as a true example."[27]

Sidney's essay is in part a rebuttal of the preface to Amyot's

27. Philip Sidney, *An Apology for Poetry,* ed. Geoffrey Shepherd (London, T. Nelson, 1965), pp. 110–111.

translation of Plutarch in which history is characterized as having "greater weight and gravity, than the inventions of the poets: because it helpeth not itself with any other thing than with the plain truth, whereas poetry doth commonly enrich things by commending them above the stars and their deserving, because the chief intent thereof is to delight."[28] Like Amyot, Fray Pedro de la Vega, the Spanish translator of Livy, contrasts history and poetry to the disadvantage of the latter, for, he says, false and fictitious tales are of no value for the attainment of honor in this world or salvation in the next.[29] Historians and their translators, of course, might be expected to praise their wares by depreciating those of others. But arguments like Sidney's failed to gain general support even among the apologists for poetry.

Professor Weinberg summarizes the views of the Italian critics: "Most critics believe that the object [of imitation] must be a true one if credibility is to result, that verisimilitude is a kind of second-best truth."[30] An audience might be persuaded to believe a fiction for the duration of a performance or a reading, but the effect could be no more than fleeting. Even so transient a success depended upon the careful avoidance of any transgression against known truth, for the structure of belief was fragile and the slightest flaw might tumble it down. And in any case, what could be more deserving of credit than truth itself? As Aeneas Sylvius (later Pius II) says in the letter to a friend which prefaces his immensely popular *De Duobus Amantibus* (otherwise known as *Eurialus and Lucretia*), "Yet shall I not, as your desire was, feign anything, nor will I there be a poet where I may be a historian. For who

28. Sir Thomas North's translation of Amyot's preface to *Plutarch.*
29. Quoted by Theodore Beardsley, Jr., in "The Classics and their Spanish Translators in the Sixteenth Century," *Renaissance and Reformation*, VIII (1971), 4.
30. Weinberg, *History of Literary Criticism in the Italian Renaissance*, I 633.

is so mad as to make use of a lie who hath a truth can justify him?[31] Or, two centuries later and more copiously, Robert Boyle in the preface to his romanticized saint's life of Theodora and Didymus: "As true Pearls are Cordials and Antidotes, which counterfeit ones, how fine soever they may appear, are not; so True Examples do arm and fortify the mind far more efficaciously, than Imaginary or Fictitious ones can do; and the fabulous labours of Hercules, and exploits of Arthur of Britain, will never make men aspire to Heroick Vertue half so powerfully, as the real Examples of Courage and Gallantry afforded by Jonathan, Caesar, or the Black Prince."[32]

The arguments of the defenders of fiction notwithstanding, the conviction persisted that a true story was one that was historically (rather than morally or philosophically) true, that it differed qualitatively from fable, and that it was superior in emotional impact and educational effectiveness. Art might indeed counterfeit nature successfully: an ancient story reported that a ventriloquist had bested a pig in a squeaking match, and Zeuxis was said to have represented grapes so naturally that birds pecked at them. But if the audience was not deceived by the artist, as the birds were, the critical question remained: how could one take seriously what one knew to be make-believe, a counterfeit of nature rather than nature itself? When, in *The Winter's Tale*, Leontes sees what he takes to be the lifelike statue of his dead wife he exclaims, "We are

31. Aeneas Sylvius, *The Historie of Eurialus and Lucretia*, tr. Charles Allen (1639), in *Short Fiction of the Seventeenth Century*, ed. Charles Mish (Garden City, N.Y., Doubleday, 1963), pp. 289–290. The Latin of the 1468(?) edition of *De Duobus Amantibus* reads: "Non tamen ut ipse flagitas. fictor ero. nec poete utemur tuba: dum licet vera referre. Quis enim tam nequam est. ut mentiri velit: cum se vero potest tueri."
32. Preface to *Theodora and Didymus* (1687), in *Prefaces to Four 17th-Century Romances*, ed. Charles Davies, Augustan Reprint Society, No. 42 (Los Angeles, University of California, William Andrews Clark Memorial Library, 1953).

mocked by art" (V.iii.68). Yet since he knows, or thinks he knows, that what he sees is art and not nature, he is not in fact deluded by art. What is strange for Leontes is that a counterfeit can produce so great an effect upon him. It is strange, too, for Francion (in Sorel's *Histoire Comique*) who is moved to wonder as he looks at a painting of the beautiful Nays: "Helas, vous n'estes rien que fiction, et pourtant vous faictes naistre en moi une passion veritable."[33] The effect of a literary fiction astonishes Hamlet:

> Is it not monstrous that this player here,
> But in a fiction, in a dream of passion
> Could force his soul so to his own conceit
> That from her working all his visage wann'd
> Tears in his eyes, distraction in's aspect
> A broken voice, and his whole function suiting
> With forms of his conceit? And all for nothing!
> (II.ii.577–583)

To the question implied by these exclamations, the Italian critic Robortello makes the obvious reply, in direct contradiction of Sidney, "If verisimilar things move us, the true will move us much more."[34]

If fiction is, as Hamlet says, merely "nothing," a counterfeit history, it can deserve no higher estimation than other counterfeits, at best to be deemed playful and recreative, otherwise vicious, absurd, or puerile, as the tales of Roland and Lancelot. The aspiring "poet" is therefore faced with a dilemma. In order to inherit the laurel of the great writers of antiquity, he must invent stories; by so doing he opens himself to the charge of frivolity. He can, to be sure, admit the charge and resort to justification on the ground that his stories

33. *Romanciers du XVIIe siècle*, ed. Antoine Adam (Paris, Gallimard, 1969), p. 352.

34. Quoted from Robortello's commentary on Aristotle's *Poetics* in Weinberg, *History of Literary Criticism in the Italian Renaissance,* I 392.

entertain, provide solace for the sick and harmless occupation for the idle. If his ambition forbids him to accept so modest a role, he may rest his claim to admiration not on the fictions which he creates but on the real values which he makes them signify or which he joins to them. Such a solution, however, reduces invented story to the status of mere adjunct or tool of the poetic faculty, rather than its essential operation. Alternatively, the storyteller may reject fictional invention, minimizing or even denying the difference between his tales and historical verity, and so assert his title to the respect that the tellers of true things generally enjoy. But adoption of this last course constitutes surrender to the historians, for those who record true events are denied the name of poet, as Servius denied it to Lucan and Ben Jonson to Du Bartas. The following chapters explore the ways in which these responses to the dilemma affected the nature and tone of Renaissance and seventeenth-century narrative.

...
iii

FICTION AS PLAY

In Renaissance times, fictional narrative was said to be time-wasting, vain, childish, trifling, frivolous, delightful, recreative, and "solacious." For some apologists, the positive epithets sufficed to redeem it. Recreation at appropriate times and for appropriate people is not an unworthy goal. The human frame is incapable of uninterrupted labor and demands its solace if it is to maintain its powers. There are those who for reasons of health or circumstance have time on their hands which cannot be spent in productive work; such time had better be devoted to harmless diversion than to sin-breeding sloth. Gentle ladies unencumbered by household duties cannot be forbidden the pleasure of listening to stories. In similar case are the very young and the very old, people in sick beds or on voyage or pilgrimage. Boccaccio protests that he undertook to write the *Decameron* for the solace of "most noble damsels," and within his fiction the ladies and gentlemen pass the time in storytelling until the plague subsides. It was so that Chaucer's pilgrims shortened the way to Canterbury. William Painter explains the title of his book of stories, *The Palace of Pleasure:* "Pleasaunt they be, for that they recreate, and refreshe weried mindes, defatigated either with painefull travaile, or with continuall care, occasioning them to shunne and avoid heavinesse of minde, vaine fantasies, and idle cogitations. Pleasaunt so well abroade as at home, to avoyde the griefe of Winter's night and length of Sommer's day, which the travailers on foote may use for a staye to ease their weried bodye, and the journeors on horsback for a chariot or lesse painful meane of travaile, instead of a merie companion to shorten the tedious toyle of wearie wayes."[1] Even Sidney, for whom poetry is the noblest of secular disciplines and fiction the heart of poetry, shares this attitude. The tales of his poet hold *children* from play and *old men* from the chimney corner, and, Sidney continues, it is the persistent childishness in grown men that makes them so receptive to imagined story.[2] He wrote his *Arcadia* when he had nothing better to do and dedicated it to his sister who had asked him to write it: "Read it then at your idle tymes, and the follyes your good judgement wil finde in it, blame not, but laugh at. And so, looking for no better stuffe, then, as in an Haberdashers shoppe, glasses, or feathers, you will continue to love the writer, who doth exceedinglie love you."[3] This light dismissal of a work on which he must have spent much labor has been explained as *sprezzatura;* it may be that, but it is surely also an example of the self-deprecation typically exhibited by those who wrote palpable fictions.

Sidney asks his sister to keep the *Arcadia* to herself or to complaisant friends: "indeede, for severer eyes it is not, being but a trifle, and that triflinglie handled." No great blame can attach to an author who wastes some time to entertain his sister or some private friends, but when he publishes for a general audience he announces his pride in the composition and subjects it to the test of worthiness. He may therefore try to avoid responsibility for publication by one means or another. Sometimes the protective screen takes the form of anonymous publication, the secret of authorship more or less well kept. Or the author may pretend that he is merely the translator of a story which he thinks is probably true though he

1. William Painter, *The Palace of Pleasure* (1566), ed. Joseph Jacobs (original edition, 1890; reprinted New York, Dover Publications, 1966), I, 13.
2. Philip Sidney, *An Apology for Poetry*, ed. Geoffrey Shepherd (London, T. Nelson, 1965), p. 113.
3. Philip Sidney, *The Countesse of Pembrokes Arcadia*, in *The Complete Works,* ed. Albert Feuillerat (Cambridge, Eng., Cambridge University Press, 1912; reprinted, 1962), I, 4.

cannot vouch for it, as Martin Fumée does when he attributes his romance *Du vray et parfaict amour* to the Greek of "Athenagoras."[4] In the case of *A Petite Pallace of Pettie his Pleasure: Contaynyng Many Pretie Hystories by him Set Foorth in Comely Colours*, the defensive device is most elaborate.[5] George Pettie's friend, one R. B., introduces the volume with an address to the gentle readers "whom by my will I would have only gentlewomen." He explains that, although the author had insisted that he keep the work to himself, his desire to delight the ladies has overcome his sense of loyalty. This letter is followed by a chronologically earlier one from Pettie to R. B. which begins, "Forced by your earnest importunity, and furthered by mine own idle opportunity, I have set down in writing, and according to your request sent unto you, certain of those tragical trifles, which you have heard me in sundry companies at sundry times report, and so near as I could have written them word for word as I then told them." Pettie prays his friend "only to use them to your own private pleasure, and not to impart them to other." Then the printer who had the book from R. B. has his say: "I fell to perusing the work, and perceived at the first by the Author's letter, that he was not willing to have it common, as thinking certain points in it to be too wanton to be wrought by that wit which by this work appeared to be in him, which as I conjecture, moved him to write to his friend to keep it private to his own use." But he has omitted some matter which the author might think offensive and so thinks it proper to publish the book though he has consulted neither R. B. nor Pettie and is not acquainted with them.

For the aspiring "poet" the goal of recreation was not enough. Authors ambitious for the garland of laurel could not rest their claim on the purveyance of glasses and feathers.

4. Martin Fumée, *Du Vray et parfaict amour escrit en Grec, par Athenagoras philosophe Athenien* (Paris, 1599).
5. George Pettie, *A Petite Pallace of Pettie his Pleasure*, ed. I. Gollancz (London, Chatto, 1908), I, 1–4.

The humanist effort to prove that the profession of letters was indispensable to the health of civilization and to the proper conduct of states and individuals gave special emphasis to the idea that literary entertainment for its own sake was a prostitution of a most noble art. A Renaissance resolution of this problem depended upon the radical dissociation of fictional narrative as such, admittedly frivolous, from the useful or admirable substance for which it might serve both as vehicle and as bait. There is nothing peculiar to the Renaissance in the contention that fiction may have purpose and meaning beyond the narration of events that never took place. It has always been possible to differentiate, speciously or not, between a tale and its emotional or intellectual implications. But it was characteristic of the Renaissance attitude I am describing to depreciate the value of the narrative component of the work, to refer to that component, with a tolerance sometimes bordering on contempt, as a concession to human weakness of no real worth save as it lured the reader to partake of the solid nourishment he might otherwise reject. This did not imply that storytelling was a matter of little moment, beneath the concern of the serious artist. To delight, even if only *in order* to instruct, remained the distinctive goal of "poetry." If the tale was to serve as an effective lure, it must be told well enough to capture and hold the attention of the audience. But the proper relationship between the author and his audience required a mutual understanding that the story was neither history told "for true" nor a childish confusion of make-believe with real, but a transparent device calculated to appeal to a less-than-serious aspect of human nature. The effect was to divide the narrative from its burden in terms of value, not merely to make a logical distinction between it and its evident implications. The division appears in its crudest form in the moralizations—often curiously irrelevant—appended to the stories in the *Gesta Romanorum* and *A Hundred Merry Tales:* "By this tale ye may learn..." In more sophisticated guise it is found also in much of the narrative literature of the sixteenth and seventeenth centuries.

Frequently, therefore, prefaces and dedications to published fiction of this period dismiss story itself as merely delightful and direct attention to the substance which justifies it. The discerning reader is urged to disclose that substance by penetrating the "dim veil" of the fiction or by interpreting particular fictitious instances as moral lessons generally applicable to real life. Or he is given to understand that the narrative was designed to provide opportunity for moral and philosophical discourses, model speeches and letters, sententious comment, descriptions, witty repartee, rhetorical displays, information about strange lands and ancient times, and other matter useful or worthy of admiration. The ways by which true value might be extracted from fictional narrative were various; among them were exemplary and allegorical interpretation (inherited by the Renaissance from classical and medieval practice), but there were many others.

In the spirit of Boccaccio's defense of poetry, Stephen Hawes asserts his intention to feign a fable in order to cloak, to draw a curtain over, to hide with a misty smoke the truth of his mind.[6] Spenser declares that he has incorporated his moral discourse into the fiction of *The Faerie Queene* because it is "the use of these dayes, seeing all things accounted by their showes, and nothing esteemed of that is not delightfull and pleasing to commune sence."[7] Until William Adlington was convinced of its allegorical meaning, he was almost dissuaded from translating Apuleius's *Golden Ass*, "fearing lest the translation of this present book (which seemeth a mere jest and fable, and a work worthy to be laughed at, by reason of the

6. Stephen Hawes, *The Pastime of Pleasure*, ed. W. E. Mead for the Early English Text Society (London, Oxford University Press, 1928), p. 6.
7. Edmund Spenser, "A Letter of the Authors," appended to the 1590 edition of *The Faerie Queene*.

vanity of the author) might be contemned and despised of all men, and so consequently, I had to be had in derision to occupy myeslf in such frivolous and trifling toys."[8] Golding accounts for his decision to translate Ovid's *Metamorphoses* on similar grounds. As the title page warns,

With skill, heede, and judgement, this worke must be read,
For else to the Reader it standes in small stead.[9]

For Aristotle, the narrative component of a tragedy or heroic poem constituted its soul; George Chapman, in defense of Homer's *Odyssey*, demotes it to the status of body:

Nor is this all-comprising Poesie phantastique, or meere fictive, but the most material and doctrinall illations of Truth, both for all manly information of Manners in the yong, all prescription of Justice, and even Christian pietie, in the most grave and high-governd. To illustrate both which in both kinds, with all height of expression, the Poet creates both a Bodie and a Soule in them—wherein, if the Bodie (being the letter, or historie) seemes fictive and beyond Possibilitie to bring into Act, the sence then and Allegorie (which is the Soule) is to be sought—which intends a more eminent expressure of Vertue, for her lovelinesse, and of Vice, for her uglinesse, in their severall effects, going beyond the life than any Art within life can possibly delineate.[10]

What is to be gained from the reading of fiction need not depend upon allegorical interpretation. Thomas Mabbe prefaces his translation of *Celestina* by describing his best readers as those who "reject the story itself, as a vain and idle subject, and gather out the pith and marrow of the matter for their own good and benefit, and laugh at those things that savour

8. William Adlington, Address to the Reader, reprinted in Apuleius, *The Golden Ass* (New York, G. P. Putnam's Sons, 1927), pp. ix–xi.
9. *Shakespeare's Ovid*, tr. Arthur Golding, ed. W. H. D. Rouse (London, Centaur Press, 1961).
10. George Chapman, *Chapman's Homer*, ed. Allardyce Nicoll (New York, Pantheon Books, 1956), II, 5.

only of wit and pleasant conceit, storing up in their memory the sentences and sayings of philosophers, that they may transpose them into such fit places as may make, upon occasion, for their own use and purpose."[11] The French translator of *Hypnerotomachia Poliphili* dedicates his work to the Conte de Nantheuil because the book treats so well of architecture that it is scarcely possible to better it.[12] Jean Maugin makes a French version of *Palmerin d'Olive* because it is "pleine d'arguments amoureux et contes de regretz lamentables (matières, au temps qui court, sur toutes autres pratiquées)."[13] Claudius Holyband sets forth an Italian version of *The Pretie and wittie Historie of Arnalt and Lucenda,* not only because of its usefulness as a first reader in Italian but also because the purchaser may "gather therein many pretie and wittie phrases, sentences, and devises, agreable to the same Argumente, and apte for the lyke or any other speache or writing."[14] To the romance *Du vray et parfaict amour,* spuriously described as a translation from the Greek, an index is added so that the reader can more readily find the rare matters and sentences contained in the volume, "avec un recueil particulier des lettres missives, harangues, & similitudes."[15] *Les Chastes amours d'Helene de Marthe* (1597) is announced, not as a story, but as "Discours contenant en termes propres offres de service, remerciemens, plaintes, instructions, songe avec l'explication, combats, duels, stratagemes, courses de bagues, danses, mascarades, description de Chasteau accompli de toutes ses parties, plaisir de volerie

11. Thomas Mabbe, in *Celestina,* ed. H. Warner Allen (London, G. Routledge and Sons, 1923), p. 4.

12. *Hypnerotomachie ou Discours du songe de Poliphile,* tr. by Jean Martin (Paris, 1546).

13. Jean Maugin, Preface to *Palmerin d'Olive* (1546), in Bernard Weinberg, *Critical Prefaces of the French Renaissance* (Evanston, Ill., Northwestern University Press, 1950), p. 133.

14. Claudius Holyband, preface to the reader in *The Pretie and wittie Historie of Arnalt and Lucenda* (London, 1575).

15. See note 4, above.

et de chasse."[16] David Rowland, dedicating his translation of *Lazarillo de Tormes* (1586) to Sir Thomas Gresham, explains that "besides much mirth, here is also a true discription of sundrie Spaniards. So that by reading hereof, such as have not travailed Spaine, may as well discerne much of the maners & customs of that country, as those that have long time continued." Sir Thomas, as one that has traveled much, can confirm this judgment.[17] The learned Jean Chapelain justifies his reading of a romance of Lancelot on the ground that though the story may be merely fabulous it nevertheless provides a true picture of the manners of the age in which it was written.[18] Embodied in a fiction, such instructive matter is made more palatable. Sir George Mackenzie's apologetic preface to *Aretina, or the Serious Romance* (1660) grants that "essayes" are the choicest pearls in the jewel house of moral philosophy, "yet I ever thought that they were set off to best advantage, and appeared with the greatest lustre, when they were laced upon a Romance."[19]

The most comprehensive assertion of the merits by which the frivolity of a work of fiction might be redeemed appears not in a preface but in the words spoken by that redoubtable enemy of chivalric romance, the Canon in *Don Quixote*. Even so absurd a genre, he declares, can be made to serve a useful purpose:

Notwithstanding all the evil he had spoken of such books, yet did he find one good in them, to wit, the subject they offered

16. Quoted by Gustave Reynier, *Le Roman sentimental avant L' "Astrée"* (Paris, A. Colin, 1908), p. 178, n. 6.
17. *The Pleasaunt Historie of Lazarillo de Tormes,* tr. David Rowland (London, 1586).
18. Jean Chapelain, *De la lecture des vieux romans* (1647), ed. Alphonse Feillet (Paris, 1870).
19. Reprinted in *Prefaces to Four 17th-Century Romances,* ed. Charles Davies, Augustan Reprint Society, No. 42 (Los Angeles, University of California, William Andrews Clark Memorial Library, 1953), p. 7.

a good wit to work upon and show itself in them; for they displayed a large and open plain, through which the pen might run without let or encumbrances, describing of shipwrecks, tempests, encounters, and battles; delineating a valorous captain with all the properties required in him—as wisdom to frustrate the designs of his enemy, eloquence to persuade or dissuade his soldiers, ripeness in advice, promptness in execution, as much valour in attending as in assaulting of an enemy; deciphering now a lamentable and tragical success, then a joyful and unexpected event; there a most beautiful, honest, and discreet lady, here a valiant, courteous, and Christian knight; there an unmeasurable, barbarous braggart, here a gentle, valorous, and wise prince; representing the goodness and loyalty of subjects, the magnificence and bounty of lords. Sometimes he may show himself an astrologer, sometimes a cosmographer, sometimes a musician, sometimes a statist, and sometimes, if he please, he may have occasion to show himself a necromancer. There may he demonstrate the subtlety of Ulysses, the piety of Aeneas, the valour of Achilles, the misfortune of Hector, the treachery of Sinon, the amity of Euryalus, the liberality of Alexander, the resolution of Caesar, the clemency and truth of Trajan, the fidelity of Zopyrus, the prudence of Cato, and, finally, all those parts that make a worthy man perfect; one whiles by placing them all in one subject, another by distributing them among many; and this being done, and set out in a pleasing style and a witty fashion, will questionless remain a work of many fair drafts, which being accomplished will represent such beauty and perfection as shall fully attain to the best end aimed at in all writing; that is, as I have said, jointly to instruct and delight: for the irregularity and liberality of those books give to the author, the means to show himself an epic, lyric, tragedian, and comedian, with all other things which the most graceful and pleasant sciences of poetry and oratory include in themselves; for epics may be as well written in prose as in verse.[20]

The formula is just that of the *Countess of Pembroke's Arcadia.*

No doubt, apologies for fiction which depended upon the instruction which might be drawn from it were sometimes

20. Cervantes, *Don Quixote,* I.47, tr. Thomas Shelton.

merely pious justifications for self-indulgence. Men had rather not admit, even to themselves, that they have been wasting their time at unprofitable occupations. It seems unlikely that the jests of *A Hundred Merry Tales* were told for the sake of their moralizations. I doubt that Arthur Brooke wrote *Romeus and Juliet* in order, as he says, to demonstrate the sinfulness of filial disobedience and auricular confession, or that Englishmen read *Lazarillo de Tormes* to acquaint themselves with Spanish customs and culture. Yet skepticism can be carried too far, as I think it is when Spenser's apology for the fiction of his *Faerie Queene* is dismissed as nothing more than advertisement. The attitude that regarded story as trivial or childish and emphasized its useful burden affected the works themselves, not merely their prefaces. Renaissance stories are typically stuffed with speeches, letters, descriptions, and similar matter. George Pettie, in fact, reduces the narrative element in the tales he retells to bald summary while he develops at large opportunities for eloquent orations, passionate epistles, and moral or mock-moral discourses. The story may even be dispensed with altogether as in the very popular "treasuries" of speeches, letters, and harangues gathered out of such stories as *Amadis of Gaul* and Belleforest's version of Bandello. The English translation of the *Amadis* "treasury" is described as "Conteyning eloquente orations, pythie Epistles, learned letters, and fervent Complayntes, serving for sundrie purposes."[21] Mlle. de Scudéry herself extracted the "conversations" from her *Clélie* and *Grand Cyrus* and published them separately, evidently with the thought that for some readers at least the delightful bait of narrative was rather a hindrance than a help.[22]

To regard fiction as play is to distinguish it from the reality

21. *The moste excellent and pleasaunt Booke, entituled: The treasurie of Amadis of Fraunce* (London, 1567). On this subject, see Reynier, *Le Roman sentimental*, pp. 254ff.

22. Madeleine de Scudéry, *Conversations sur divers sujets*, 2 vols. (Paris, 1680).

it mimics. Of course, if a game is to be interesting it must be related to reality closely enough to engage normal human responses. But when the distinction between make-believe and real is obscured—when disbelief is shut out rather than suspended or held back—a voice from the balcony calls out to warn the stage heroine of the approach of the villain. Novelists since Richardson have striven for effects of this kind, if not of this naïveté. Our sense of the nature of fiction has developed from that tendency of the novel that Ian Watt calls "formal realism." Once we have opened the pages of a novel we do not wish to be reminded that the events recorded are not true history. For the space of our reading we expect to be captivated, to find the characters "convincing," the plot (however fantastic) within its terms believable. Henry James accuses the author who betrays the unreality of his story and so breaks his own bubble of committing "a terrible crime."[23] Watt, similarly, judges Fielding's ironic attitude toward his fiction a grave fault;[24] no doubt he finds Nabokov's tone blameworthy too. Despite the seriousness of the transgression, storytellers not infrequently commit it. Shakespeare is so bold as to remind his audience that the actor playing the part of Polonius is not Polonius at all but the actor who once played the part of Julius Caesar—at a London theater, surely, rather than at the university of the fiction.

When the Gentleman in *Winter's Tale* says that the news of King Leontes' finding his long-lost daughter "is so like an old tale, that the verity of it is in strong suspicion" (V.ii), the effect must be to confirm the impression that the story is indeed of the kind told to children by the fireside. If such reminders prick the illusion, they may, paradoxically, enhance its

23. Henry James, "The Art of Fiction" (1884), reprinted in *Selected Literary Criticism: Henry James*, ed. Morris Shapira (New York, Horizon Press, 1964), p. 51.

24. Ian Watt, *The Rise of the Novel* (Berkeley and Los Angeles, University of California Press, 1965), pp. 285ff.

meaning. In a kind of Persian painting, an equestrian scene is surrounded by a painted frame into which intrude the tail and hoof of one of the horses. The frame so emphasized identifies the scene as an artistic composition and so divides it from real life. But at the same time as the intrusion of hoof and tail denies the reality of the artistic conception, it underscores its relevance to the large, real world outside.

Renaissance makers of fiction, despite James and Watt, seek to delight or instruct their readers, not to delude them. They do indeed write passages of vivid description—rhetorical *enargeia*—and they prize the contrivance that can make impossible things seem so credible that the reader's mind, held in suspense, is ravished with delight and wonder. Representation of reality is scarcely a major concern, however, and the fictional character of the tale is not really in doubt. Recognition that the story is play and not history lies at or near the surface of awareness, not deep beneath it, for the author parodies the role of historian rather than assumes it, and he does not want his reader to think him so unscrupulous as to tell false for true or so foolish as to play a child's game with the seriousness of a child. If he presents himself as one who reports things that have happened, his attitude is like that of a masker at a fancy dress ball who hopes that the audience will admire the art of his dress and his acting but certainly not mistake him for the character he is playing. As Federico remarks in the second book of *Il Cortegiano*, a young man who masquerades as an old one should so clothe himself as to betray the nimbleness of his person.

Many narratives of the period, in fact, are not credible at all, though they may be entertaining and most artistically wrought. The action is often minimal or of little consequence, events succeeding each other, not in a march to an end but because they offer suitable occasions for instructive or admirable discourse. The narrative road does not proceed to its destination; rather it twists and turns because what is important is by the way. The traveler is constantly being asked to suspend his journey in order to contemplate one or another object of interest. If he is impatient to find out what happened, he will find little but frustration in such notable (and very various) fictions of the age as Sannazaro's *Arcadia, Orlando Furioso, Diana Enamorada, Gargantua, Don Quixote, Jack Wilton, The Faerie Queene, L'Astrée*. Some of these are crowded with interwoven tales while others have scarcely any action, but none is a coherent narrative designed to capture the reader's belief by the moving force of a causally determined sequence of events, and in none is the reader tempted to think that he is reading about things that have happened.

So far are some makers of Renaissance fiction from desiring to create a convincing illusion of reality that, like Castiglione's masquerading courtier, they go about deliberately to sabotage it and to poke fun at those so simple as to entertain it. Like Bottom, they must make sure that the ladies do not mistake make-believe for real. Not only should there be an explanatory prologue but the player must thrust his head through the lion's skin and say, "If you think I come hither as a lion, it were pity of my life. No, I am no such thing; I am a man as other men are" (*Midsummer Night's Dream*, III.i). Shakespeare toys here with the absurd notion that so knowledgeable an audience as the court of Theseus could be as naïve as the Athenian mechanicals thought them. By so doing, he invites the people in the theater not to lose themselves in the fictitious action but to sit apart from it and to become, like Theseus and his companions, tolerant, amused observers of childish antics —the antics not only of Bottom and his friends playing Pyramus and Thisbe but also of the young lovers and of mortal actors in the theater of the world.

What Bottom and his friends do naïvely, the sophisticated presenters of fiction do jocularly. Like More, Rabelais, Cervantes, and others, they may resort to the device of mock-serious assertion of the truth of an obviously fictitious story.

Such jokes flatter the audience by assuming its intelligence; at the same time they emphasize the fictionality of the tale, its parodic rather than imitative relation to the real world. Or the author may let his audience see the strings by which he manipulates his puppets, as Ariosto does when he explains that he will release Bradamante and Ruggiero from their enchantment when the time serves—for the present his desire for variety requires him to change the subject.[25] Nashe, too, makes his Jack Wilton assert the "signiory" of his pages—whether the reader will or no he will do with his story as the mood moves him.[26]

The tale may be made to undermine itself. At the extreme, this becomes outright burlesque, as when we are told that Pantagruel transported into Dipsody "a colony of Utopians to the number of 9,876,543,210 men, besides the women and children."[27] Of course, since it is only at odd moments that we can believe at all in what happens in Rabelais's story, the report of this population movement does not really mock our credulity. That does happen, however, when the story is plausible enough to engage some fraction of belief and then oversteps the bounds. On the assumptions of *Orlando Furioso*, Ruggiero's flying horse is no unnatural phenomenon, but we boggle when Orlando spits six enemies on his spear and then discards the weapon because it can hold no more.[28] We may accept More's Utopians even when they dig a channel to divide their land from the neighboring continent, but not when we read of their using gold for chamber pots, or when we find that newly hatched Utopian chicks follow men and women instead of hens. In Machiavelli's *Belphagor* we do not think it incredible that the privy council of Hell should depute Pluto

25. Ariosto, *Orlando Furioso*, XIII.80.
26. Thomas Nashe, *The Works*, ed. R. B. McKerrow, 2nd ed. (Oxford, Blackwell, 1958), II, 227.
27. Rabelais, *Gargantua and Pantagruel*, III.1.
28. Ariosto, *Orlando Furioso*, IX.68.

to investigate the complaint that earthly marriage is the principal cause of human damnation, but we are brought up short by the remark that Pluto's wife "had taken Physick that week and kept her Chamber."[29] Most ingenious is Cervantes' device of introducing Don Quixote to the duchess who has read all about him in the printed Spanish version of the ancient Arabic account of his adventures.[30]

Unlike most long fictions of the age, the original version of Sidney's *Arcadia* is a well-constructed narrative in which each incident has its causes and consequences, the whole moving toward an end foreshadowed at the beginning. Interspersed, to be sure, are debates and orations on such topics as the duties of kingship, the antagonism of reason and love, and the nature of life after death, and action comes to a full stop during the pastoral interludes which divide the books. But even such interruptions do not altogether impede the movement of the tale. If this sequential quality is indeed a virtue, Sidney thought so little of it as to abandon it almost completely in his revision, for the newly invented matter so overwhelms the basic story that the reader often quite forgets Basilius' desertion of the rule of Arcadia and the courtship of the two young heroes for the lovely princesses.

Despite its coherence, the *Old Arcadia* is not designed to create an illusion of reality. Sidney ruins that illusion, even at critical points of the story. The rescue of the beautiful Philoclea from the jaws of a ravening lion by the enamored Pyrocles, disguised as an Amazon, has all the ingredients of high drama. But when Pyrocles engages the beast as it is about to devour the lady he cries out wittily, "Are yow become my Competitour!" And then, carrying the lion's severed head, he pursues the still-fleeing Philoclea, but not so eagerly as to catch up with her because "her light Nimphlyk apparell beeyng carryed

29. Machiavelli, *The Works*, anon. tr. (London, 1680), p. 524.
30. Cervantes, *Don Quixote*, II.30.

up with the wynde, that, muche of those beutyes shee woulde at an other tyme have willingly hidden, were presented to the eye."[31]

The heightened manner of the revised *Arcadia* multiplies effects of this kind. The original version includes an account of Musidorus' fight again the "Rascall Company" that interrupts his attempt to rape Pamela.[32] In the revision Sidney builds this into a full-scale burlesque of the assault made by the rebels upon Basilius' pastoral retreat: "Yet among the rebels there was a dapper fellowe, a tayler by occupation, who fetching his courage onelie from their going back, began to bow his knees, & very fencer-like to draw neere to *Zelmane*. But as he came within her distance, turning his swerd very nicely about his crown, *Basilius*, with a side blow, strake of his nose. He (being a suiter to a seimsters daughter, and therefore not a little grieved for such a disgrace) stouped downe, because he had hard, that if it were fresh put to, it would cleave on againe. But as his hand was on the grounde to bring his nose to his head, *Zelmane* with a blow, sent his head to his nose..."[33] In terms of the political teaching of the *Arcadia* the episode dramatizes the serious proposition that a leaderless realm must degenerate into chaos. But Sidney's account is so grotesquely "witty" that all sense of danger is lost and the reader is left to laugh—that is, if his sensibilities permit. Indeed, Sidney is so much more interested in writing admirably than in telling his story that his artifice deliberately rejects the world as it is. Philoclea and Pamela "impoverished their cloathes to inriche their bed"[34]—imagine Richardson's Pamela so preparing herself for the night!

Our pleasure at the turn of Sidney's words depends in part on his playful exaggeration of the beauty of fictional heroines.

31. Sidney, *Arcadia*, in *Works*, IV, 43.
32. *Ibid.*, IV, 287–288.
33. *Ibid.*, I, 312.
34. *Ibid.*, I, 176.

Even our ears, made gross by centuries of cultural change, can sometimes detect such notes; no doubt we are deaf to much more. At least it can be said that parody is a remarkably common mode in the Renaissance: *Orlando Furioso* and *Don Quixote* mock the chivalric tradition; *The Praise of Folly*, the rhetorical; *Gargantua*, the stories of giants; *Utopia*, the travelers' tales. None of these is merely parody, and in all but the *Orlando*—perhaps I should not except it—the light fiction is made to carry a burden of weighty matter. This did not trouble contemporary readers, but it does confuse modern ones; the debate continues as to whether these works are witty entertainments or grave discourses. That they can be both at once seems to be hard for the modern reader to accept. Our critical assumptions demand that the relationship between narrative body and meaningful soul be compatible, that vehicle be appropriate to tenor, the mood of the one consonant with that of the other. Evidently such considerations weighed less heavily with Renaissance storytellers. In the following chapter I explore this theme with regard to a work of fiction whose tone, I think, has often been misapprehended: Edmund Spenser's *The Faerie Queene*.

iv

HOBGOBLIN AND
APOLLO'S GARLAND

To Drayton's "grave moral" and Milton's "sage and serious" Spenser I would add, not altogether as a footnote, a playful one. The idea that whatever is comic about *The Faerie Queene* is so despite its author no doubt continues to prevail. Yet at least since the time of Upton some readers have been moved to laugh with Spenser rather than at him, and in recent years the response has been common enough to generate a number essays with such titles as "Spenser's High Comedy," "His Earnest unto Game: Spenser's Humor in *The Faerie Queene*." "Spenserian Humor: *Faerie Queen III and IV*," and a doctoral dissertation called "The Comedy of *The Faerie Queene*."[1]

1. Among recent studies which discuss Spenser's humor at some length, in one or another of its aspects, are the following: Harry Berger, "Spenser's 'Faerie Queene,' Book I: Prelude to Interpretation," *Southern Review: An Australian Journal of Literary Studies*, II, Pt. 1 (1966), 18–49; Judith Petterson Clark, "His Earnest unto Game: Spenser's Humor in 'The Faerie Queene'," *The Emporia State Research Studies, Medieval and Renaissance Studies*, XV, no. 4 (1967), 13–24, 26–27; Martha Craig, "The Secret Wit of Spenser's Language," *Elizabethan Poetry*, ed. Paul Alpers (New York, Oxford University Press, 1967), pp. 447–472; Judith Dundas, "Allegory as a Form of Wit," *Studies in the Renaissance*, XI (1964), 223–233; Robert O. Evans, "Spenserian Humor: Faerie Queene III and IV," *Neuphilologische Mitteilungen*, LX (1959), 288–299; A. H. Gilbert, "Spenserian Comedy," *Tennessee Studies in Literature* II (1957), 95–104; Clyde G. Wade "The Comedy of The Faerie Queene," unpub. diss., University of Missouri, Columbia, 1967 (*Dissertation Abstracts* 28.3651A–52A); W. B. C. Watkins, *Shakespeare and Spenser* (Princeton, N.J., Princeton University Press, 1950), Note I: "Spenser's High Comedy (Faerie Queene 2, 3)," pp. 293–

It has even been proposed that mirthlessness is the quality not of the poet but of his scholarly commentators. Perhaps the wind is shifting.

I am indebted to these studies for many of the examples I shall cite. But I am concerned particularly with the kind of playfulness in which the player mocks his own role. Much of what is remarked as humorous in *The Faerie Queene* is an integral part of its fictional stuff. When, for example, Spenser makes fun of Braggadocchio or shows us those fair ladies vainly trying to put on the girdle of chastity the comedy arises within the story: the characters are ridiculed, but the tale is not. I wish here to draw attention to Spenser's jesting, not at the characters and their actions but at his own fiction, mockery deliberately designed to undermine the narrative illusion. The difference between the two kinds of jest is like that between our laughter at and with Falstaff, in whom we do believe, and our laughter at Chaucer's Sir Thopas, in whom we do not. Of course, *The Faerie Queene* is not an outright burlesque like "The Tale of Sir Thopas." But there is burlesque in it, and recognition of that quality should temper and refine our reading of the poem. Spenser's story is indeed enchanting, like a child's fairy tale or a fantastic dream, yet it is a child's tale told to mature and sophisticated adults, a dream in broad daylight. Spenser's friend, the learned Gabriel Harvey, returned an early draft of the poem to him with the comment that it seemed Hobgoblin had run away with the garland from

---

304; Arnold Williams, *Flower on a Lowly Stalk* (East Lansing, Mich., Michigan State University Press, 1967), pp. 113–120. An unpublished and undated essay on the subject by Charles Bell Burke is preserved at the library of the University of Tennessee. The first chapter of a projected book to be entitled "The Comic Element in Spenser," it surveys in considerable detail the opinions of Spenser's critics regarding his sense of humor, or lack of it. Burke did publish a note entitled "The 'Sage and Serious' Spenser," *Notes and Queries*, 175 (1938), 457–458.

Apollo.[2] I think Hobgoblin stands for the fanciful fiction, Apollo's garland for the meed of a deeply moral poet writing in the great heroic tradition. I am here concerned only with Hobgoblin. I take as my text the comment of R. W. Church in the English Men of Letters series: "It has been said that Spenser never smiles. He not only smiles with amusement or sly irony; he wrote what he must have laughed at as he wrote, and meant us to laugh at."[3]

What he wrote was a heroic poem of high moral purpose, certainly not a laughing matter for the Renaissance. But it was also a narrative fiction dealing with brave knights' and ladies' gentle deeds, a tale typical of what Dean Colet called the "blotterature" of ignorant and misguided ages. In the glow of Renaissance self-esteem, chivalric story was an absurd, dead fashion, worthy only of such mocking uses as Ariosto made of it. "King Arthur's knights long since are fled," wrote Thomas Howell in 1581[4] Thomas Nashe described stories of this genre as "the fantasticall dreames of those exiled Abbie-lubbers, from whose idle fantasticall pens proceeded those worne out impressions of the feyned no where acts of Arthur of the rounde table, Arthur of litle Brittaine, sir Tristram, Hewon of Burdeaux, the Squire of low degree, the foure sons of Amon, with infinite others."[5] The editor of Spenser's *Shepheardes Calender* condemned the inventors of those "no where acts" as "fine fablers and lowd lyers."[6] Ascham accused them of immorality, and Sidney's tutor warned against the

2. *The Works of Edmund Spenser, A Variorum Edition. The Prose Works* (Baltimore, Md., Johns Hopkins Press, 1949), p. 472.

3. R. W. Church, *Spenser* (London, Macmillan, 1906; 1st ed., 1879), p. 141.

4. Quoted by Charles Bowie Millican, *Spenser and the Table Round* (Cambridge, Mass., Harvard University Press, 1932), p. 183, from *Howell His Devises* (1581).

5. Thomas Nashe, *The Anatomie of Absurditie,* in *The Works,* ed. R. B. McKerrow (Oxford, Blackwell, 1958), I, 11.

6. "April" gloss.

reading of "vile & blasphemous, or at lest of prophan and frivolous bokes, such as are that infamous legend of K. Arthur."[7] Sidney himself was rather more indulgent, for in defense of fiction he argued that *Orlando Furioso* or "honest King Arthur would be more pleasing to a soldier than a discourse concerning the quiddity of *ens*.[8]

There was, certainly, a species of subliterature in verse, prose, and in the theater which continued in all seriousness the tradition of the chivalric tale into the Renaissance and beyond. Its stubborn persistence in this kind is exemplified by the continuing popularity of *The Most Illustrious and Renowned History of the Seven Champions of Christendom*, the first part of which was first published in 1596. I have an edition—it is called the eighteenth, which must be an understatement— printed in Wilmington, Delaware, in 1804. It is in three parts, "Containing their honourable Births, Victories and noble Atchievements, by Sea and Land, in divers strange countries; their combats with Giants, Monsters, &c. Wonderful Adventures in Desarts, Wildernesses, inchanted Castles; their Conquests of Empires, Kingdoms; relieving distressed Ladies, with their faithful Loves to them: the Honor they won in Tilts and Tournaments, and success against the Enemies of Christendom." The description is perfectly appropriate to the narrative of *The Faerie Queene*.

Spenser, nevertheless, elected this outmoded kind of story for his most ambitious undertaking. He had good reasons for doing so, some of which he lists himself. The example of Vergil taught him, as it taught Ronsard, to choose his hero from his nation's ancient past. Arthur's name was known to all, yet so little was recorded about him historically, particularly before

7. Quoted by Josephine Waters Bennett, *The Evolution of "The Faerie Queene"* (Chicago, University of Chicago Press, 1942), p. 75, from Nathaniel Baxter's dedication to his translation of Calvin's *Sermons* (1578).

8. Philip Sidney, *An Apology for Poetry*, ed. Geoffrey Shepherd (London, T. Nelson, 1965), p. 127.

his accession to the throne, that the poet was free to make fictions, precisely the activity that defined him as a poet. "Fierce warres and faithfull loves" provided appropriate metaphors for the conflicts and attractions central to the moral problems with which he was concerned. And despite such mockery and abuse as I have cited, the chivalric tradition carried with it an atmosphere of golden antiquity, of "beautiful old rhyme / In praise of ladies dead and lovely knights." (If not *The Faerie Queene* what could Shakespeare have been thinking of?) Samuel Daniel would have others "Sing of Knights and Palladines / In aged accents and untimely words / Paint shadowes in imaginary lines, / Which well the reach of their high wits records."[9] Queen Elizabeth's Accession Day festivities continued to honor, at least ceremonially, the outworn ritual of tilt and tournament. In later centuries, the influence of *The Faerie Queene* itself and the search for some equivalent of the moribund pastoral made of the tales of ladies, of knights, and their impossible adventures a kind of golden literary world. But the ambivalence of Renaissance attitudes with respect to the chivalric tradition is illustrated dramatically in Shakespeare's *Troilus and Cressida* when noble Hector's storybook challenge to single combat for the honor of a fair lady provokes both admiration for a knightly gesture and Achilles' comment, " 'Tis trash."

Spenser is not like Shakespeare's Achilles, but he too recognizes the absurdity of chivalric narrative and from time to time exposes it to his own amusement and that of his readers. He confronts literary convention with the world as it is, not by means of guffaw, but by a subtle use of devices common to all burlesque, hyperbole, bathos, and patent illogic. That many passages in *The Faerie Queene* are hyperbolic, bathetic, and illogical, few would deny. The question remains, however, whether they are so because of the poet's naïveté or because of his sophistication. It is not a question that can be answered

9. Samuel Daniel, *Delia*, Sonnet XLVI.

definitively, for it is not given to us to recapture fully the mood
in which a work centuries old was written and read. Furthermore, the attempt to answer it is by its nature self-defeating.
All dissection injures its subject, and of all subjects literary
tone must be the most delicate. Who has ever laughed at a
dissected joke?

A test case may serve to focus the issue. In the course of the
climactic battle between St. George and the dragon, a battle
fraught with the most profound moral and religious significance, the knight wounds his adversary under the wing:

> Forth flowed fresh
> A gushing river of blacke goarie blood,
> That drowned all the land, whereon he stood;
> The streame thereof would drive a water-mill.
> (I.xi.22)

In the Ovidian battle which Spenser appears to have been
imitating, the monster's hemorrhage merely dyes the grass
red. (*Metamorphoses,* III.85–86.) Does Spenser's passage lie
within the fictional convention of desperate encounters, so
that the hyperbole of the bloody river and the incongruity of
the water mill are not parody but failure of taste, or is he mocking that convention at the same time as he makes use of it?
If Chaucer were the author, the question would be easy to resolve. In the "Knight's Tale" the sworn friends Palamon and
Arcite agree to settle their competition for the love of Emily by
mortal combat. They chivalrously arm each other and then
chivalrously hack at each other. Perhaps this teeters on the
boundary between fictional gallantry and burlesque of it. The
story continues:

> Up to the ancle foghte they in hir blood.
> And in this wise I lete hem fightyng dwelle,
> And forth I wole of Theseus yow telle.
> (ll.1660–2)

The blood tide is rather too high, the transition too abrupt. We
are not disposed to take "Up to the ancle foghte they in hir

blood" as inept hyperbole because we know that Chaucer is neither stupid nor lacking in a sense of the ridiculous. Nor can we dismiss the "Knight's Tale" as mere burlesque, like the "Tale of Sir Thopas." In the delicate balance that Chaucer achieves, the reader accepts the chivalric convention at the same time that he recognizes its absurdity. But Spenser's reputation labors under those heavy Miltonic epithets. He is a self-confessed allegorist dedicated to a moral purpose, a method and end we have been taught to regard as grimly humorless. The contrast of *The Faerie Queene* with *Orlando Furioso* reinforces our prejudice: the English poet borrows episode and rhetoric from the Italian but not his mood, and sometimes he seems to miss or (as I think) to ignore Ariosto's jokes. We read the *Orlando* as a delicious Renaissance entertainment; because *The Faerie Queene* is so very different, some critics are led to think of it as a late flowering of a decayed tradition rather than as a poem of the High Renaissance deliberately dressed in an outworn fashion.

In fact, much of Spenser's poetry is conceived as though it were by somebody else—as Professor Harry Berger neatly puts it, written in quotation marks. The pompous lugubriousness of *The Teares of the Muses*, the rusticity of language and rudeness of rhythm of *The Shepheardes Calender*, the simplicity of the shepherds of *Colin Clouts Come Home Againe* are surely dramatically assumed poses. There is not, I think, any self-mockery in these; rather, we are asked to admire the skill with which the poet plays his roles. In the *Amoretti* the invented speaker is Spenser himself posing as conventional sonneteer. Professor Louis Martz has remarked not only on the consciously artificial nature of that pose but also upon Spenser's subtle parody of it.[10] In Sonnet LIV, Martz points out,

10. Louis Martz, "The 'Amoretti': 'Most Goodly Temperature,' " *Form and Convention in the Poetry of Edmund Spenser*, Selected Papers from the English Institute, ed. W. Nelson (New York Columbia University Press, 1961), pp. 146–168.

Spenser speaks directly of his playing diverse pageants in the world's theater and complains that, whether he "mask in myrth" or make his woes a "tragedy," his lady merely mocks. Surely the reader is invited to react similarly—to mock, though not merely.

Among the many voices of *The Faerie Queene* is one which tells its story as though it were written by a poet of long ago, ancient and therefore good, simple, and credulous, a lover of the fair and the brave. Often this speaker does not fully understand the tale he tells; sometimes he distorts its meaning. His language is marked by archaisms, his story by the clichés of medieval romance. He is not unlike the figure of the poet Gower whom Shakespeare puts forward as the "presenter" of *Pericles*—that "mouldy" tale as Ben Jonson called it. Behind this poet-narrator stands Spenser himself, making his presence felt from time to time in order to remind the reader that he has only suspended his disbelief, that the tale of heroes and heroines, monsters and witches, however profound its significance may be, is nevertheless only a tale. This he does typically in those passages in which the story is most characteristically old-fashioned.

Among the most conspicuous features of medieval narrative is its pretense that it is indeed historically true, based upon authoritative documents or reports. Rabelais mocks this pretense in *Gargantua;* Boiardo and Ariosto, in their *Orlando*s; More, in *Utopia;* Cervantes, in *Don Quixote*. Professor Robert Durling remarks on humorous pseudodocumentation in Boiardo and Ariosto, but Spenser, he says, "uses the mention of supposed sources of the poem . . . to lend authority, plausibility, or an aura of antiquity to the story—never for humorous effect."[11] Like most absolutes, I doubt that this one can be sustained. The key passage in which Spenser defends the

11. Robert Durling, *The Figure of the Poet in Renaissance Epic* (Cambridge, Mass., Harvard University Press, 1965), p. 224.

historical truth of his story is the Prologue to Book II. As More had done before him, Spenser pretends to be disturbed by the idea that some readers may doubt his veracity:

> That all this famous antique history,
> Of some th'aboundance of an idle braine
> Will judged be, and painted forgery,
> Rather then matter of just memory.

He is forced to admit that the "antiquities" he cites as authority are hard to come by. Yet the Amazon River and Virginia really were there before they were found, and other populated regions, perhaps even those in outer space, no doubt await other explorers. Therefore, he argues, Fairyland exists because it has not yet been discovered. The logical absurdity should warrant at least a smile.

Sometimes the reader is invited to verify the truth of the tale himself. Should he happen by the region of Merlin's cave (its location is precisely given though not easy to find) he must not attempt to enter its recesses "For feare the cruell Feendes should thee unwares devowre" (III.iii.8). Rather, Spenser advises, he should put his ear to the ground so that he can hear the dreadful noises within. A similar effect is produced by the testimony to the historical reality of Arthur's sword. After Arthur's death, we are told,

> the Faerie Queene it brought
> To Faerie lond, where yet it may be seene, if sought.
> (I.vii.36)

Had the poet stopped with "where yet it may be seene" the reader might well have taken it as the usual coin of chivalric narrative designed, as Durling suggests, to lend an aura of antiquity to the story. But the addition of "if sought" must make him wonder how to go about the seeking.

No chivalric tale can properly be without its desperate encounters between knight and knight or knight and horrid beast. Sparks fly, armor plate is riven, blood flows in torrents. There are many such battles in *The Faerie Queene,* and C. S. Lewis thinks that Spenser does this kind of thing very badly.[12] But perhaps that usually admirable critic failed to distinguish between bad writing and something that verges on parody. I let pass the dragon's blood-operated water mill, for some may think it intended seriously. But there can be no difference of opinion about Corflambo's recognition of his defeat by Arthur:

> ere he wist, he found
> His head before him tombling on the ground.
> (IV.viii.45)

Or Artegall's conquest of Grantorto:

> Whom when he saw prostrated on the plaine,
> He lightly reft his head, to ease him of his paine.
> (V.xii.23)

Or Britomart's overthrow of Sir Scudamour:

> to the ground she smote both horse and man;
> Whence neither greatly hasted to arise,
> But on their common harmes together did devise.
> (IV.vi.10)

Or Radigund's escape from Artegall's huge stroke:

> had she not it warded warily,
> It had depriv'd her mother of a daughter.
> (V.iv.41)

Or the desperate fight between that virago and Britomart:

> [they] spared not
> Their dainty parts, which Nature had created
> So faire and tender, without staine or spot,
> For other uses, then they them translated;
> Which they now hackt and hewd, as if such use
> they hated.
> (V.vii.29)

12. C. S. Lewis, *The Allegory of Love* (Oxford, Oxford University Press, 1936; reprinted 1958), p. 347.

Mocking the precision of a grocery clerk, Spenser says that the maw of the Blatant Beast has the capacity of "A full good pecke within the utmost brim" (VI.xii.26). Orgoglio's yell of pain when Arthur cuts off his left arm is likened, oddly enough, to the bellow of a herd of sexually excited bulls (I.viii.11). A few stanzas after the amputation of that left member the giant returns to the fray:

> The force, which wont in two to be disperst
> In one alone left hand he now unites.
>
> (I.viii.18)

Evidently Spenser is lightheartedly willing to undermine with a pun the seriousness of these combats even though they must signify the desperate struggles of the soul.

The most desperate of these is surely that of the Red Cross Knight against the powers that would destroy him. The subtle Archimago is a formidable magician indeed, capable of transforming himself into a dragon, of course, but also into fish, fowl, or fox, forms so terrifying

> That of himselfe he oft for feare would quake,
> And oft would flie away.
>
> (I.ii.10)

And the story of the final battle with the satanic dragon—that in which the water mill passage occurs—is handled no more respectfully. If one wishes to find a prime example of the comparison of great things to small, there can be few more striking instances than the likening of the "well of life" which can restore the dead and wash away the guilt of sinful crime to the "English *Bath* and eke the german *Spau*" (I.xi.30). When the newborn knight rises from immersion in that well he wounds his adversary with his sword, hardened, Spenser suggests, by holy water dew. The dragon, dazed and terribly angered, roars and renews the attack:

> Then gan he tosse aloft his stretched traine,
> And therewith scourge the buxome aire so sore,
> That to his force to yeelden it was faine.
>
> (I.xi.37)

The "buxome" gives it away. No doubt the obedient air did yield, as it does to the tail of my kitten.

Other examples of what must be deliberate bathos and incongruity are easy to find. The cosmic challenge of Mutability to the principle of constancy in the world takes the form of a motion at law, so that the ruler of Olympus is constrained to bid Dan Phoebus (who here becomes court clerk) to "Scribe her Appellation seale" (VII.vi.35). The list of "idle fantasies" that flit in the chamber of Phantastes in the House of Alma includes supernatural creatures, beasts, birds, and human beings graded in anticlimax:

> Infernall Hags, *Centaurs*, feendes, *Hippodames*,
> Apes, lyons, Aegles, Owles, fooles, lovers, children,
> Dames.
>
> (II.ix.50)

The cannibal nation, having made captive the sleeping Serena, debates as to whether to eat her at once or let her sleep her fill, deciding on the latter course by cookbook logic: "For sleepe they sayd would make her battill [fatten, as for the table] better" (VI.viii.38). When the naked girl is rescued at the critical moment by Sir Calepine, she says not a word to him. Her silence Spenser explains by describing her mood as "unwomanly" (VI.viii.51). As for Calepine himself, since the great work by Calepino was so well known to all Europe that his name had become a common noun, he must have meant "dictionary" or "thesaurus" to Spenser's reader, rather more specifically than "Webster" does to us. I do not quite get the force of this joke, but it must be a joke because among the other characters in this sixth book are Aldus and his son Aldine, as who should say, Sir Clarendon Press.

Storybook ladies are of course incomparably beautiful, and Spenser's are no exception. Since the poet tells us that in some places Belphoebe shadows the Queen herself, the highest reach of praise is called for. Yet, as Watkins remarks,[13] it may be even beyond that reach to say that the double pleasure of sight and smell provided by the roses and lilies of Belphoebe's face is "Hable to heale the sicke and to revive the ded" (II.iii.22). A few stanzas later in this blazon the hyperbolic mood is suddenly broken: "Below her ham her weed did somewhat traine" (II.iii.27). I am not absolutely sure about that "ham." Its primary meaning is "the back of the knee" and Spenser uses the word again in describing the way the Amazon Radigund tucks up her dress in order to free herself for action. Still, it is not a word one expects to find in an encomium on the beauty of so noble a lady as Belphoebe.[14] And what is one to make of Spenser's choice of simile for her legs:

> Like two faire marble pillours they were seene,
> Which doe the temple of the Gods support,
> Whom all the people deck with girlands greene,
> And honour in their festivall resort.
>
> (II.iii.28)

The marble pillars derive from the Song of Solomon, but the bedecked temple which they support appears to be Spenser's addition. The comparison is only less curious than that produced for Serena's "goodly thighes":

> whose glorie did appeare
> Like a triumphall Arch, and thereupon
> The spoiles of Princes hang'd, which were in battel won.
>
> (VI.viii.42)

13. Watkins, *Shakespeare and Spenser,* p. 300.
14. Shakespeare uses the word "ham" in *Romeo and Juliet* II.4.57; *Hamlet* II.2.203; and *Pericles* IV.2.114, always in reference to men and always in derogation.

No doubt the poet wished to suggest the awestruck admiration
which the sight of those legs and thighs would arouse. But if
the descriptions were written in all seriousness, would he have
made the response so ceremonially public?

Jests based on physiological function and so-called "kitchen"
subjects seem particularly inappropriate for so elevated a discourse as *The Faerie Queene*. The reference to the natural uses
of the dainty parts of Britomart and Radigund is therefore
startling, but it is not unique. A comprehensive anatomy of
the House of Alma—the human organism—must inevitably
include a description of its service rooms, but the kitchen of
this generally well-ordered establishment seems to me so volcanically overheated as to require radical remedy:

> in the midst of all
> There placed was a caudron wide and tall,
> Upon a mighty furnace, burning whot,
> More whot, then *Aetn'*, or flaming *Mongiball*.
> (II.ix.29)

And the section devoted to this digestive subject ends with
puns not demanded by Spenser's moral purpose:

> all the rest, that noyous was, and nought,
> By secret wayes, that none might it espy,
> Was close convaid, and to the back-gate brought,
> That cleped was *Port Esquiline*, whereby
> It was avoided quite, and throwne out privily.
> (II.ix.32)

Even the daintiest of storybook ladies, Spenser reminds us,
must on occasion suffer just such inconveniences as ordinary
people do. Britomart having fallen asleep, the lovely Amoret
leaves the security of her protector's martial prowess and
walks through the wood, "for pleasure or for need" (IV.vii.4).
There is nothing inherently funny about the circumstance
that Amoret should "for need" go off into the woods. The joke
is at the expense not of the girl but of the narrative illusion

itself—the fictional lady is here confronted by one with the usual complement of digestive organs. Here, and in the other passages I have been citing, what is within the fictional frame is faced directly or implicitly by what is without. The result is not as catastrophic as the confrontation of the Snowy Flori-well by the true one. The fiction does not melt away as the witch's creation does; rather it stands revealed for what it is, attention having been drawn to the fact that it is an illusion.

Overt jests at the expense of the fiction are not to be found in every stanza or in every canto of *The Faerie Queene*. They are nevertheless common enough to warn the reader that the naïveté of the narrator is a deliberately assumed pose, that Spenser is playing a part and expects his audience to know it. Nowhere does this mock naïveté appear more strikingly than in the story which is formally (though in form only) the prin-cipal action of the whole poem, the enamorment of Prince Arthur and his quest for Gloriana, Queen of the Fairies (I.ix.8–15). If Spenser was to pose as a medieval storyteller, what better choice of tale could he have made than one so typically medieval that Chaucer made fun of himself by telling it? Arthur's resemblance to the absurd Sir Thopas is unmis-takable. Both chastely reject love; both on a day ride out hunting. Arthur is "prickt forth with jolitee of looser life"; Thopas pricks forth both north and east and falls into a love-longing. For Arthur, all nature laughs; for Thopas the herbs spring and the birds sing. Both weary of their sportful prick-ing and dismount to lie down on the soft grass. Arthur uses his helmet as pillow, an uncomfortable practice which Chau-cer tells us (though not in the immediate context) is also Thopas'. The Prince dreams that the Queen of Fairies lies down beside him and makes him "Most goodly glee and lovely blandishment." Sir Thopas has a similar dream: a fairy queen shall be his leman and lie beneath his cloak. On waking, both heroes resolve to find their dream loves and their search takes them both to the country of Faery. And nothing more is heard of either quest. Though both poems are aborted, surely for different reasons, each has room for development of the story but neither makes use of it. In Spenser's version Chaucer's tail rhyme—"drasty ryming" (as the Host calls it)—is turned into the Spenserian stanza; obvious banalities are eliminated. Yet although the new version surely signifies the seductive power upon noble youth of a dream of glory, the story itself remains puerile, the characters unrealized, the events barely recounted, their sequence unmotivated. Since we recognize the similarity of the tale of Arthur's dream to that of Sir Thopas, many of Spenser's contemporaries must also have recognized it.

For some modern readers it is intolerable to believe that the central action of a poem of such manifest seriousness as *The Faerie Queen* could derive from a patent joke. Yet Spenser not only read "Sir Thopas," but he read it attentively, for he refers to Thopas and the giant Ollyphant elsewhere in his poem, and in his treatise on Ireland he discourses learnedly, though no doubt erroneously, on the resemblance of Thopas' costume to the dress of Irish horsemen.[15] One scholar attempts to resolve the dilemma by suggesting that Spenser took Chaucer's tale in dead earnest; lacking humor himself, he found no humor in it. Another concludes that since "Thopas" is funny, Spenser's source must have been some other medieval story, no doubt one of the kind that Chaucer burlesques. Another argues that, since the tale of Arthur's enamorment plainly derives from "Sir Thopas," it must be the residue of an earlier draft of *The Faerie Queene,* one without pretensions to didactic purpose and written at the time Spenser was proposing to "overgo" Ariosto rather than to fashion a gentleman or noble person in virtuous and gentle discipline. But it is inconceivable that any normally intelligent adult could take

15. Edmund Spenser, *A View of the Present State of Ireland,* lines 2177ff.

Chaucer's story seriously, almost as inconceivable as that a scholar should think that he did. Similar tales are of course to be found in medieval literature—why else should Chaucer have ridiculed them?—but Spenser had no need to seek elsewhere for his matter. And whether or not the story of Arthur's falling in love and vowing his great quest is part of the debris of an earlier version of *The Faerie Queene*, the poet did include it in the work which he presented so proudly to Queen Elizabeth. If narrative of this kind is what Gabriel Harvey objected to when he described that draft of the poem that Spenser sent him in 1580 as "Hobgoblin runne away with the garland from Apollo" the criticism still holds for the work as we have it. Spenser's imitation of the Thopas story, coupled with his mocking use of the clichés of chivalric narrative, leads to the conclusion that he found nothing incompatible in the association of an absurd tale and a deeply moral significance.

As Curtius shows, the Middle Ages did not doubt that jest and earnest could live together.[16] Prudentius finds it appropriate for St. Lawrence on the gridiron to suggest to his executioners that since he has been cooked on one side they have the opportunity of deciding whether the rare or the well-done is more savory. Hagiographers enliven their accounts of the saints with reports of how they miraculously make broken bottles whole or end a plague of insects by excommunicating them. In heroic poetry, too, comedy had its license, given authority by Servius' judgment that the story of Dido in the fourth book of the *Aeneid* is almost wholly comic in style, naturally, says Servius, since its subject is love. To Curtius' medieval examples I would add a Renaissance one: the episode in Canto IX of Camoens' *Lusiads* which concerns the delicious isle on which Thetys and her nubile nymphs provide

16. E. R. Curtius, *European Literature and the Latin Middle Ages*, tr. W. R. Trask (New York, Pantheon Books, 1953), Excursus IV.

sexual reward for the comically eager sailors of Vasco da Gama's heroic expedition. Camoens explains at last that the isle is not an isle and the nymphs not nymphs:

> For these fair Daughters of the Ocean,
> Thetys and the Angellick pensil'd Isle,
> Are nothing but sweet Honour, which These wan;
> With whatsoever makes a life not vile.
> The priviledges of the Martial Man,
> The Palm, the Lawrell'd Triumph, the rich spoile;
> The Admiration purchac't by his sword;
> These are the joys, this Island doth afford.
>
> (IX.89)[17]

The equation of sexual satisfaction with "sweet Honour" and "Lawrell'd Triumph" is exactly that of Arthur's dream of Gloriana.

Much of the harshest criticism of *The Faerie Queene* arises from its failure to meet expectations bred by the tradition of the novel. Spenser's stories do not hang together very well, narrative threads are left untied, episodes succeed each other apparently at haphazard, characters lack recognizable humanity. To counter such charges, one apologist invokes a theory of successive careless revisions. Another attempts to discover a formal dramatic structure in the text, a construction I doubt it will bear. Yet another accounts for the inconsequence of the narrative by describing *The Faerie Queene* as a dream poem, and indeed the story has the apparent formlessness of a dream without the excuse that its maker is asleep. Some single out Britomart as truly flesh and blood, usually on the ground that she undergoes a jealous tantrum, but I am not convinced, for all that, that she is tangible. *The Faerie Queene* is not of the genre of *Pamela, War and Peace,* or even Tolkien's *Lord of the Ring.* As the poet declares in his letter to Ralegh, he has

17. Luis de Camoens, *The Lusiads,* tr. Sir Richard Fanshawe, ed. Geoffrey Bullough (Carbondale, Ill., Southern Illinois University Press, 1963).

embodied his instruction in a fiction because the example of great poets has sanctioned it and because it is "the use of these days" to demand delightfulness. But he is quite aware, and wants the reader to be quite aware, that the tale is merely a tale, an old-fashioned and most improbable one. Hence the note of parody and burlesque which deliberately breaks into the narrative enchantment.

The parodic quality in the narrative of *The Faerie Queene* is quite different from that of *Orlando Furioso*. Unlike Spenser's poem, Ariosto's could never be misunderstood, even by the dullest reader, for a straightforward example or imitation of the tradition it burlesques. Spenser's reader is indeed absorbed, as the poet himself claims to be, by that delightful land of Faery. But it can be delightful only if he does not really believe in those awful monsters, witches, and bloody combats. So from time to time he is nudged awake, though only tentatively, for the transitions are almost imperceptible, the narrative flow resumes, and the wounded illusion heals itself. Those moments should suffice, I think, to remove him just so far from the fiction that he is at once seduced by it and amused by his own seduction. Perhaps such a mood is set by the deliberately quaint "pricking" and "yclad" of the very first lines of the first canto. If the play of diction is so responded to, the reader will not trouble to inquire how that poor lamb kept pace with the Red Cross Knight and Una; nor will he feel inclined to suppose that, since it is never seen again, Una must have cooked it for supper.

$\mathcal{V}$

THE FLIGHT FROM FICTION

The defense of fiction which made of it a delightful means to an admirable end—body for a meaningful soul, vehicle for valuable freight—was open to easy challenge. For the mature, or for those who thought themselves mature, such means were needless; grown men could take what was good for them without the childish dilution of sugar water, so that, Spenser concedes, some "had rather have good discipline delivered plainly in way of precepts, or sermoned at large, as they use, then thus clowdily enwrapped in allegoricall devises."[1] And there were skeptics who doubted the validity of the appeal to the example of the poets of antiquity. Bacon, like Rabelais before him, came to the conclusion that Homer "in his own meaning" intended no such figural inwardness by his fables as later expositors drew from them.[2]

The condemnation of fiction as frivolous and vain was given added emphasis by post-Renaissance tendencies. Puritanism and the Counter-Reformation were at one in their intolerance of frivolity, and, as Professor Russell Fraser has shown, the newly powerful bourgeoisie had only contempt for the time-wasting toys of the effete.[3] In *Musophilus*, Samuel Daniel makes the worldly Philocosmus say of poetic invention:

> Other delights than these, other desires
> This wiser profit-seeking age requires[4]

1. Edmund Spenser, "A Letter of the Authors," appended to the 1590 edition of *The Faerie Queene.*
2. Francis Bacon, *Advancement of Learning,* II.iv.4.
3. Russell Fraser, *The War Against Poetry* (Princeton, N.J., Princeton University Press, 1970), esp. chap. iii.
4. Samuel Daniel, *Musophilus,* lines 12–13.

To accommodate those desires, the storyteller was tempted to reject the purely fictional subjects elected by his predecessors of the sixteenth century, Ariosto, Rabelais, Ronsard, Sidney, Spenser. He sought, instead, a way of making his tale in some sense historical and so acquiring for it the unquestioned praises of history, while at the same time maintaining his claim to the distinctive poetic function of "making." The compromise, inevitably an uneasy one, took a variety of forms. He might exaggerate or elaborate a historical matter, giving "poetic" development to the truth of the basic plot. He might incorporate the fictional narrative in a historical setting and make his invented characters take part in veritable actions. He might declare his tale to be no fiction at all but a narration of true events under a veil of feigned names and altered circumstances. Or he might assert the story to be a true one indeed, but of a kind that historians failed to tell—a tale of people of no fame or political significance.

Such blending or confusion of fiction and history was encouraged by the absence of a clear distinction between them, especially when history was understood as historians practiced it, rather than as the naked truth they professed it to be. Despite their pretenses, historians were ignorant of many things, they disagreed with each other, they were partisan, they were given to conjectures as to causes and motives. Those who followed the classical tradition invented speeches and concocted descriptions. Histories were therefore by no means free of fiction; in fact they differed from it not in kind but only in the quantity of invention, so that many of them should really be classed, Roger Boyle says, as "mixed romances."[5]

Nor was historical truth altogether alien to "poetry." Although Aristotle had noted the *Flowers* of Agathon as an ex-

5. Roger Boyle, Preface to *Parthenissa*, in *Prefaces to Four Seventeenth Century Romances*, ed. Charles Davies, Augustan Reprint Society, No. 42 (Los Angeles, University of California, William Andrews Clark Memorial Library, 1953).

ample of pure fiction, he had also made the point that, since things that happen are clearly possible, if they are also probable they become suitable subjects for the poet. There were thought to be seeds of historical truth in the Homeric poems and in the *Aeneid*, though admittedly much was fable and some (like the story of Dido and Aeneas) clearly false. Too much verity, to be sure, ruined the poetic character of the work, as the example of Lucan's *Pharsalia* made clear. For Ronsard, therefore, a little truth sufficed: a real cottage could be made into a poetic palace, a spark into a blazing fire.[6] But others, like Tasso, felt the need for more historic substance, though of such kind as to permit the poet liberty to invent without contradicting what was known to be true.

In taking for his subject the crusaders' conquest of Jerusalem Tasso rejected Ariosto's example of the wholly fictional heroic poem. As poet rather than historian he did invent characters and episodes and made use of the established machinery of the epic, supernatural intervention and all. But he found it necessary to apologize to his muse for daring to mix Parnassian fictions with the truth; the heavenly muse, he declares at the outset, does not deck her brows with fading bays by the Heliconian spring.[7]

Other narrative poets reduced still further the fictional element in their tales. Unlike their great classical models, they chose subjects in which "witte's inviron'd in with veritie,"[8] recent history or Biblical story. The choice of a "true" subject did not of itself signal a rejection of fictional ones: Sir David Lindsay, writing of his own knowledge about his heroic contemporary Squire Meldrum, compares him with Lancelot as to morality, which suggests that he made no great difference

6. Pierre de Ronsard, Preface to the edition of 1587, in *Oeuvres complètes*, ed. P. Laumonier (Paris, Hachette, 1950), XVI, 340.

7. Torquato Tasso, *La Gerusalemme liberata*, Canto I, stanza 2.

8. John Weever, sonnet commending C. Middleton's *Legend of Humphrey Duke of Gloster* (1600).

between the two as to reality.[9] But other poets deliberately emphasized their avoidance, more or less complete, of fiction. Although Camoens includes frankly fabulous episodes and supernatural machinery in his celebration of the voyage of Vasco da Gama, he boasts to the King of Portugal of the essential truth of his story, so making his matter, if not his poem, better than Ariosto's:

> Hear me, I say, for not for Actions vaine,
> Fantastick, Fabulous, shall you behold
> Yours prais'd, though forraigne Muses (to obtaine
> Name to themselves) have ev'n feign'd names extold.
> Your Subjects true Acts are so great, they staine
> And credit all the Lyes of others told;
>   Stain Rhodomont, that puffe Rogero too,
>   And Mad Orlando, though their deeds were true.[10]

And Camoens' translatator, Fanshawe, declares that the *Lusiads* differs from the work of all other poets who "wrought in great," whether ancient or modern: "For (to name no more) the Greek Homer, the Latin Virgil, our Spencer, and even the Italian Tasso (who had a true, a great, and no obsolete story, to work upon) are in effect wholly fabulous: and Lucan (though worthily admired) is as much censured by some on the other side, for sticking too close to truth."[11] For Agrippa d'Aubigné the Heliconian spring feigned by the Greeks no longer runs as once it ran; the waters now are red with the real blood of Protestant martyrs:

> Ces ruisselets d'argent, que les Grecs nous feignoyent,
> Où leurs poëtes vains beuvoyent & se baignoyent,
> Ne courent plus ici: mais les ondes si claires

9. David Lindsay, *Squyer Meldrum*, ed. James Kinsley (London, T. Nelson, 1959), ll.48–52.
10. Luis de Camoens, *The Lusiads*, tr. Sir Richard Fanshawe, ed. Geoffrey Bullough (Carbondale, Ill., Southern Illinois University Press, 1963), Canto I, stanza 11.
11. *Ibid.*, p. 52.

Sont rouges de nos morts: le doux bruits de leurs flots
Leur murmure plaisant heurte contre des os.[12]

Samuel Daniel chides himself (and no doubt Edmund Spenser) in the words of the ghost of Henry V:

Why do you seeke for fained *Palladines*
(Out of the smoke of idle vanitie)
Who may give glory to the true designes,
Of Bourchier, Talbot, Nevile, Willoughby?
Why should not you strive to fill up your lines,
With wonders of your owne, with veritie?
T'inflame their ofspring with the love of good,
And glorious true examples of their Blood.

What everlasting matter here is found,
Whence new immortall *Illiads* might proceed!
That those, whose happie graces do abound
In blessed accents, here may have to feed
Good thoughts; on no imaginarie ground
Of hungry shadowes, which no profite breed;
Whence, musicke-like, instant delight may growe;
Yet, when men all do knowe, they nothing knowe.[13]

Desmarets is happy to have found in the history of Clovis the kind of marvelous matter that Ariosto, Tasso, and other heroic poets were forced to invent.[14] Bernard Lesfargues, author of *David, poème heroique,* proudly rejects that art which teaches how to feign and lie with impunity.[15] Cowley asserts that his *Davideis* will

unbind the charms that in slight Fables lie,
And teach that Truth is truest Poesie.[16]

12. Agrippa d'Aubigné, *Les Tragiques,* I, "Misères," ll. 59–64.
13. Samuel Daniel, *Civil Wars,* V.4, 5.
14. Jean Desmarets, *Clovis, ou la France Chrestienne* (Paris, 1657), Sig. e 4ʳ.
15. Quoted by R. A. Sayce, *The French Biblical Epic in the Seventeenth Century* (Oxford, Clarendon Press, 1955), p. 106.
16. Abraham Cowley, *Poems,* ed. A. R. Waller (Cambridge, Eng., Cambridge University Press, 1905), p. 243.

Milton's admiration for the ancient heroic poets and for Spenser may have kept him from so forthright a rejection of fiction as Cowley's. But his final abandonment of the subject of Arthur for his epic poem is plausibly explained by his doubts of its historical truth, and he does declare that it is not in his nature

> to dissect
> With long and tedious havoc fabled knights
> In battle feigned[17]

—the argument he has chosen is a higher one. And something more than polemical heat leads him to condemn "the polluted orts and refuse of *Arcadia's* and *Romances*" and to describe Sidney's work as a "vain amatorious Poem," however witty.[18]

The open conventionality and artificiality of dramatic performance should suffice, one might think, to insulate the theater from the demand for truth. As Sidney says, "What child is there that, coming to a play, and seeing *Thebes* written in great letters upon an old door, doth believe that it is Thebes?"[19] It may be, as Brome has it, that "True Stories and true Jests do seldom thrive on Stages."[20] Yet the recurrent vogues of the chronicle play and drama based on contemporary incident are obviously responses to the desire for factual narrative, and the number of times that the word "true" appears on the title pages of Elizabethan and Jacobean printed plays testifies to its value as advertisement. *Selimus* is announced as "No fained toy nor forged Tragedie," and the audience of *Henry VIII* is warned not to expect an intermix-

17. John Milton, *Paradise Lost,* IX.30–31.

18. John Milton, *Eikonoklastes,* in *The Works* (New York, Columbia University Press, 1931–1940), V, 86–87.

19. Philip Sidney, *An Apology for Poetry,* ed. Geoffrey Shepherd (London, T. Nelson, 1965), p. 124.

20. Richard Brome, *Jovial Crew,* V.1.

ture of "fool and fight" with the "chosen truth" which is its subject. In France, the epilogue to Théodore de Bèze's *Sacrifice d'Abraham* (1576) asserts

> Ce ne sont point des farces mensongeres,
> Ce ne sont point quelques fables legeres:
> Mais c'est un faict, un faict tresueritable
> D'un serf de Dieu, de Dieu tresredoutable[21]

And Jean de la Taille similarly prefaces his *Saül le Furieux* (1572): "Je n'ay des histoires fabuleuses mendié icy les fureurs d'un Athamant, d'un Hercules, ny d'un Roland, mais celles que la verité mesme a dictées, et que portent assez sur le front leur sauf-conduit partout." He goes on to beg the stoic censor's indulgence for the few liberties which he has taken with the Biblical text, liberties which he justifies as having at least verisimilitude and the shadow of truth.[22] George Chapman's defense of the fictions in *The Revenge of Bussy d'Ambois* is more truculent: "And for the autentical truth of either person or action, who (worth the respecting) will expect it in a poem, whose subject is not truth, but things like truth?"[23]

Poets and dramatists had a great classical body of fiction for precedent; those who wrote stories in prose did not. The notable examples of classical prose are historical, philosophic, rhetorical, or didactic; ancient prose fiction familiar to Renaissance writers is represented by only a scattering of very various works, none of them of the stature of the *Aeneid* and most subject to the accusation of frivolity: the Greek romances, Xenophon's *Cyropedia*, Lucian's *True History*, the Aesopic fables, Apuleius's *Golden Ass*, the *Satyricon* of Petronius Arbiter. Since rhyme was proverbially alternative to reason and

21. Quoted by Bernard Weinberg, *Critical Prefaces of the French Renaissance* (Evanston, Ill., Northwestern University Press, 1950), p. 152.
22. Quoted *ibid.*, pp. 229–230.
23. George Chapman, *The Revenge of Bussy d'Ambois*, dedication to Sir Thomas Howard.

poetry the father of lies, prose should naturally be the vehicle of rationality and truth, a medium for instruction and for informing the present of what had transpired in the past.

Prose was, nevertheless, the medium chosen by most writers of fiction as it had been increasingly during the later Middle Ages. For the Renaissance and after, the principal classical model was the Greek romance, the example of which bred a numerous progeny including Sidney's *Arcadia* and its English followers, John Barclay's Latin *Argenis*, and the very long-winded romances of the first half of the seventeenth century in France. Since Renaissance critics assimilated this kind of story to the genre of the epic, they allowed its right to be called heroic poetry in prose and so validated its claim to admiration. Typically, these tales begin *in medias res* with a sensational and mysterious incident; they present a principal action (though there are many subordinate ones also); their heroes are pious, brave, and gentlemanly Aeneases. Unlike the *Ethiopian History* and Sidney's *Arcadia*, the French romances are usually given historical settings worked out in more or less detail, and they incorporate historical actions. In romances published after 1640, the historical matter tends to grow in importance, even to the point of dominating the action. Maurice Magendie remarks that this development parallels a similar tendency in the contemporary drama.[24] The romance writers are sensitive to the charge of falsifying the past and often insist that they do not contradict the historical known, or that they deviate from any one historian no more than other historians do.[25] Calprenède protests: "In effect, I can truly say that in the

24. Maurice Magendie, *Le Roman français au XVIIe siècle* (Paris, E. Droz, 1932, reprinted Geneva, Slatkine Reprints, 1970), p. 130. For generalizations concerning the French romances I am indebted particularly to Chapter IV, "La Conception du roman dans la première moitié du XVIIe siècle."
25. See A. J. Tieje, *The Theory of Characterization in Prose Fiction prior to 1740*, University of Minnesota Studies in Language and Literature 5 (1916), p. 18.

Cassandre and the *Cléopâtre* not only is there nothing contrary to truth, though there may be things beyond truth; but also that there is no passage in which one can convict me of lying, and that through all the circumstances of the History, I can prove it as true when I please. I shall add nothing of my own to the matters of importance."[26]

The relation of fiction to history in the romances is nevertheless quite different from that in the *Lusiads* or Drayton's *Mortimeriados*. In those poems, the fiction enhances and interprets the history; in the romances, history subserves the fiction. In the preface to *Ibrahim*, Scudéry recalls Strabo's judgment that "a man will lie more plausibly if he will mix in some actual truth": "When as falshood and truth are confounded by a dexterous hand, wit hath much adoe to disentangle them, and is not easily carried to destroy that which pleaseth it, contrarily, whenas invention doth not make use of this artifice, and that falshood is produced openly, this gross untruth makes no impression in the soul, nor gives any delight."[27] And an interlocutor in one of the "conversations" in Scudéry's *Clélie* remarks that the age chosen for the setting of a fiction should be such that the reader might well believe that historians had failed to mention the story, but it should not be so distant and unfamiliar as to create a sense of unreality.[28] That Gomberville chose history for the sake of the fiction rather than the other way about is clear from the curious case of his *Polexandre*. The version published in 1629 (*L'Exil de Polexandre*) is set in the latter half of the sixteenth century and includes a brief history of the Peruvian Incas and an account of the naval battle of Lepanto. A revised version, pub-

26. Quoted from the Preface to *Faramond, ibid.,* p. 21.
27. Madeleine de Scudéry, Preface to *Ibrahim*, tr. Henry Cogan (London, 1674), in *Prefaces to Fiction*, ed. Benjamin Boyce, Augustan Reprint Society, No. 32 (Los Angeles, William Andrews Clark Memorial Library, 1952).
28. Quoted by Thomas F. Crane in the Introduction to his edition of Boileau's *Les Héros de Roman* (Boston, Ginn and Company, 1902), pp. 118–119.

lished three years later, is set in the eighth century, substitutes Persians for Incas and, as the hero of the battle, the Emperor Justinian II for Don John of Austria. In a prefatory note Gomberville remarks that some readers disliked the change because they found the more modern setting more entertaining. He himself is partly of their opinion, but he will defer to majority judgment. In 1637, still another version of the romance appeared, this time set in the early sixteenth century.[29]

The romances, then, were primarily fictional, but, curiously, their fictions might turn out to be history after all. Some readers, says Charles Sorel, praise romances for their inventions, and some for their style, but there are also those who esteem them for one reason only, that is because they relate true happenings under feigned names.[30] Whether by the intent of their authors or by the interpretation of others, the romances were very often read as disguised accounts of contemporary men and affairs, so that with the proper key one could discover verities. The key may appear on the title page: "La Galatée et les adventures du prince Astiages, histoire de nostre temps, où sous noms feints sont representez les amours du roy et de la reyne d'Angleterre, avec tous les voyages qu'il a faits tant en France qu'en Espagne."[31] Sir Robert Le Grys appends such a key to his translation of Barclay's *Argenis:*

To give what contentment I am able, to the commendable curiosity of such, as out of a work of such a raised conceit and stile, are desirous to draw what profitable knowledge they possibly may, not slightly passing it over as an idle Romance, in which there were no other fruit conteined, but fantasticall tales, fit onely to put away the tediousnes of a Winter evening; I have, as farre as my coniecture would reach, helped by my acquaintance with the passages of this latter Age, both in our

29. See Philip A. Wadsworth, *The Novels of Gomberville, a Critical Study of Polexandre' and 'Cytherée'* (New Haven, Yale University Press, 1942), chapter ii.
30. Charles Sorel, *La Bibliothèque françoise,* 2nd ed. (Paris, 1667), p. 187.
31. Cited by Magendie, *Le Roman français,* p. 249.

owne and our neighbour Countries, annexed to this my Translation this Key. Wherewith, the Reader may unlocke the inten-
tions of the Author in so many parts of it, as I could conceive
he had any aime in at all.[32]

Jean Pierre Camus explains that a story in his *Agathonphile*
tells of a contemporary affair about which he has certain
knowledge. He has transported it from France to Rome and
dressed it in antique fashion, using the liberty common to
rhetoricians, poets, and painters.[33] Sir Kenelm Digby writes his
autobiography in the form of a romance, assigning to himself
the name of Theagenes and to his wife Lady Venetia Stanley
that of Stelliana. Thomas Wilson, translating Montemayor's
Diana in 1596, is sure that neither that work nor Sidney's
Arcadia is a simple fiction: "Wherein under the names and
vailes of sheppards and theire Lovers are covertly discoursed
manie noble actions & affections of the Spanish nation, as is
of the English of that admirable and never enough praised
booke of Sir Phil. Sidneyes Arcadia."[34] No doubt, the persistent
(and often misguided) attempts of modern scholars to discover
history or autobiography under the veil of old fictions spring
from a similar conviction that there must be more historical
substance to them than appears on the surface.

In a comment on Barclay's *Argenis*, Clarimond in Sorel's
Lysis challenges the very conception of the *roman à clef*: "Why
should we love truth better under a vail then when she is
naked?[35] A defense is offered by a translator of Scudéry's *Grand*

32. *Iohn Barclay his Argenis*, tr. Sir Robert Le Grys (London,
1629), p. 485.
33. Jean Pierre Camus, *Agathonphile ou les martryrs Siciliens*
(Paris, 1621), p. 853.
34. "Diana de Monte Mayor Done out of Spanish by Thomas
Wilson (1596)," manuscript edited by Henry Thomas, *Revue His-
panique*, L (1920), 367–418.
35. Charles Sorel, *Lysis*, tr. J. Davies under the title *The Extravagant Shepherd* (London, 1653?), Sig. I ii 1ʳ: Bk. 13, "The Oration
of Clarimond against Poetry, Fables, and Romances."

Cyrus: "For the Intrigues and Miscarriages of War and Peace are better, many times, laid open and Satyriz'd in a *Romance,* than in a downright History, which being oblig'd to name the Persons, is often forc'd for several Reasons and Motives to be too partial and sparing; while such disguis'd Discourses as these, promiscuously personating every Man, and no Man, take their full liberty to speak the Truth."[36] But if the veil was thin enough to be transparent, that liberty disappeared, as Bussy-Rabutin discovered when his privately circulated *L'Histoire amoureuse des Gaulles* fell into the hands of a printer: the consequence was thirteen months in the Bastille and exile for life to Burgundy.[37] Sorel remarks that authors of *romans à clef* risked not only legal punishment but also the private vengeance of the individuals concerned.[38] In view of such inconveniences, it is not surprising that some storytellers sought other ways to accommodate the preference for verity over the verisimilar.

The heroic poems, the chronicle and Biblical plays, and many of the romances combine in various ways and in various proportions fictional and historic ingredients. The fiction may be intended to make the history vivid, to interpret it, to draw a lesson from it, or to disguise it; the history may lend an air of credibility to the fiction or provide an excuse for reading it. Not infrequently, the author announces that he has mingled the two components or, like Tasso and Jean de la Taille, apologizes for having done so. He may even challenge the reader to disentangle them. In the preface to his *Parthenissa* (1655), Roger Boyle, Lord Broghill, distinguishes his tale from earlier

36. The translator's preface to Scudéry's *Artamène ou le Grand Cyrus* in *Novel and Romance 1700–1800, A Documentary Record,* ed. Ioan Williams (New York, Barnes and Noble, 1970), p. 25.
37. Antoine Adam, *Histoire de la littérature française au XVIIe siècle* (Paris, Domat, Montchrestien, 1948–1956), IV, 175.
38. Charles Sorel, *La Connoissance des bons livres* (Amsterdam, 1673), p. 187.

English romances on the ground that they were purely fabulous while his contains much of truth: " 'Tis like Ore in which the Refyner will have Drosse and Mettle." But he will not identify the historic metal "since that might silence a Curiosity, the raising whereof is one of my cheefest ends in writing this Booke."[39] Others are less teasing. Boursault explains that the martial parts of his *Prince de Condé* are historically true, the amatory invented.[40] The account of Caesar's invasion of Britain in William Warner's *Albion's England* is interrupted by "amidst our serious penne, this Fable entertaine."[41] Elsewhere, Warner feels free to enliven the history with invented tales, no doubt with the expectation that his readers will distinguish the fiction by its manner. Indeed, the title page of the book announces that the poem is an "Intermixture of Histories and Invention." Familiarity with the conventional licenses claimed by historians and poets would have made certain kinds of matter immediately recognizable as invented: soliloquies, verbatim accounts of conversations, such episodes as those in Shakespeare's *Henry VI*, Part III, in which a nameless father kills his son and a nameless son his father. How audiences understood Prince Hal's escapade on Gadshill or the scene in *Henry VI*, Part I, in which the Countess of Auvergne tries to trap Talbot is hard to know; perhaps some members of them took those fictions for history.

For those who had a high regard for historical truth, its mixture with fiction was intolerable, for the consequence was not to make the history interesting or the fiction credible but to sully the truth. This was emphatically the case when the historical matter was Biblical, and there were violent attacks

39. See note 5, above.
40. *Le Prince de Condé par feu M. Boursault* (Paris, 1739): "On peut regarder comme autant de verités les endroites qui ne concernent que la Guerre, mais on ne garantit pas ceux où l'Amour a quelque part."
41. William Warner, *Albions England*, 3rd ed. (1592), Sig. I 4ʳ.

upon the use of such subjects for drama and heroic poetry.[42] If only fictions based upon Biblical story had been so criticized, the influence of Reformation and Counter-Reformation attitudes might be thought paramount. But the status of fictionalized secular history was also becoming dubious. By the seventeenth century, historians had begun to resign their classical privilege of inventing speeches and describing battle scenes; the gap between their métier and that of the "poets" had widened to the point where one could no longer mix the genres without qualms. Because such miscegenation involves true history in "a thick Darkness," the encyclopedist Pierre Bayle believes the time has come for the authorities "to give these new Romance-Makers their Option; either to write clean History, or pure Romance; or at least to use Crotchets to separate Truth from Falshood."[43] In fact, as early as 1566, Luis Zapata had been scrupulous enough to mark off the invented passages in his *Carlo Famoso* with just such "crotchets."[44]

42. E. K. Chambers, *The Elizabethan Stage* (Oxford, Clarendon Press, 1923, reprinted with corrections, 1951), IV, 211, quotes "Anglo-phile Eutheo" (Anthony Munday?), 1580: "The reverend word of God & histories of the Bible, set forth on the stage by these blasphemous plaiers, are so corrupted with their gestures of scurrilitie, and so interlaced with uncleane, and whorish speeches, that it is not possible to draw anie profite out of the doctrine of their spiritual moralities." John Field (1583) is quoted (*ibid.*, p. 222): "The word of our Salvation, the price of Christ his bloud, & the merits of his passion, were not given to be derided and jested at, as they be in these filthie playes and enterluds on stages & scaffolds, or to be mixt and interlaced with bawdry, wanton shewes, & uncomely gestures, as is used (every Man knoweth) in these playes and enterludes." Sayce (*The French Biblical Epic*, p. 18) cites Pierre le Moyne as condemning the combination of invention (*mensonge*) with sacred truth.

43. Pierre Bayle, *An Historical and Critical Dictionary* (London, 1710), *s.v.* "Nidhard." On this subject, see Herschel Baker, *The Race of Time* (Toronto, University of Toronto Press, 1967), pp. 81ff.

44. Luis Zapata, dedication to *Carlo Famoso* (1566), quoted by E. C. Riley, *Cervantes' Theory of the Novel* (Oxford, Clarendon Press, 1962), p. 168.

Samuel Daniel seems to have been increasingly affected by a sense of the impropriety of the mixture of fact and fancy: from the historical fiction of his *Complaint of Rosamund* (1592) he moves to the *Civil Wars* (1595), a poem in which he declares "I will not poetize," and then to the *Collections of the Historie of England* (1612), a prose work in which Daniel restricts himself to the ascertainable past.

If fictional dross could not be justified by admixture of historical metal, the inventor of stories might seek recourse to the pretense that he was indeed a historian and not a "poet" at all. Throughout the Middle Ages, storytellers had maintained the fiction that they wrote no fiction, but it was an old device, one which had become a subject for jest, and the sharpened sensitivity of audiences to the difference between history and fiction had made them more inquisitive as to the truth of reported actions. Nevertheless, if the tale was circumstantially documented and neither improbable nor in conflict with the known, the question as to its verity could have no certain answer.

Although new information about the past did turn up from time to time—manuscripts had been discovered and forgotten books dug out of library shelves—when a story concerned famous men and told of great actions which had not previously been recorded it was no doubt suspect. In some cases, such inventions were soon laid bare. Guevara's *Libro de Emperador Marco Aurelio* (1529) pretends to be a translation of an ancient biography discovered in the library of Cosimo de Medici, "an impudent forgery," C. S. Lewis rather harshly calls it.[45] Its falsity was discovered during Guevara's lifetime. Sir Thomas Elyot describes his *Image of Governance* (1541) as a translation of a life of the Emperor Alexander Severus written by his secretary Eucolpius, supplemented (since Elyot had to

45. C. S. Lewis, *English Literature in the Sixteenth Century Excluding Drama* (Oxford, Clarendon Press 1954), p. 150. See Bayle, *An Historical and Critical Dictionary*, s.v. "Guevara" and "Rua."

return that book to its owner) by material from other authentic sources.[46] In fact, about one-third of Elyot's text derives from Lampridius (in the *Historiae Augustae Scriptores*), and the remainder is fiction. By the seventeenth century, the *Image of Governance* was recognized as a fraud, or as a victim of fraud.[47] Few historians, even of their own time, put much faith in the "secret histories" and "chroniques scandaleuses" derived, so their seventeenth- and eighteenth-century authors claimed, from manuscript memoirs, diaries, and family traditions. Yet it is not always possible to distinguish fiction from history. The authenticity of the hugely popular *Letters of a Portuguese Nun* has from time to time been challenged, but though the evidence against it is strong it remains inconclusive.[48]

The falsified history of a public figure can often be exposed by its conflict with other sources of information or rendered doubtful by the absence of corroborative evidence, but the tale of people of no fame outside of their own localities is almost invulnerable to contradiction, particularly when the author says that he has altered the names or the setting or both for the sake of *bienséance* and to protect the persons involved or those connected with them. A great many such stories were written during this period. In their concern with ordinary people in contemporary settings rather than with princes in Samarkand they resemble the novellas which, as commentators of the period remark, are more like history than the ro-

46. *Four Political Treatises by Sir Thomas Elyot,* facsimile ed. (Gainesville, Florida, Scholars' Reprints and Facsimiles, 1967), pp. 205–206.

47. See John Selden, *Commentarii Eutychii Aegyptii, Patriarchae Orthodoxorum Alexandrini* . . . (London, 1642), Sigs. Yy3ᵛff.

48. *Les Lettres portugaises* (1669), translated into English by Sir Roger L'Estrange (1678). The English version reached a tenth edition by 1740. See Natascha Würzbach, *The Novel in Letters* (Coral Gables, Florida, University of Miami Press, 1969), p. 3.

mances.[49] But while the typical novella may make a token assertion of its truth, it asks for tolerance rather than for belief. The pseudohistorical tale insists upon its verity; the story is not only true but known to almost the whole world; there are more than a dozen witnesses to the affair; it is a most veritable history, so recent that everyone knows of it; it is based on a truth testified to by the author's own eyes and ears; it is no fiction of Cupid and Psyche but the history of the writer's own passion.[50]

As it is difficult to prove "domestic" stories of this kind false, so it is difficult to persuade the reader that they are true. Since the witnesses cannot be interrogated nor the manuscripts examined, the narrative must testify to its own truth, must be so like the truth that it can be no other. Verisimilitude in this sense is an affirmative quality quite different from the avoidance of impossibilities and improbabilities. Not merely the action but the reporting of the action must be constrained by the limitations of the world as it is, and this requires the testimony of a narrator (whether he bear the author's name or that of some other) whom the audience can be induced to trust. The narrator can tell only what he can probably know, either as one present at the events or as a recipient of information about them. It is not likely that he has heard a character soliloquize and taken the text down verbatim or that he

49. P. J. Yarrow, *A Literary History of France*. II, *The Seventeenth Century 1600–1715* (London, Benn, 1967), p. 289, quotes Segrais, *Nouvelles françoises* (1656): "Au reste il me semble que c'est la différence qu'il y a entre le Roman et la Nouvelle, que le roman écrit ces choses comme la bienséance le veut, et à la manière du Poète; mais la Nouvelle doit un peu davantage tenir de l'histoire et s'attacher plutôt à donner les images des choses comme d'ordinaire nous les voyons arriver, que comme notre imagination se les figure." See also William Congreve, Preface to *Incognita* (1692).

50. For examples, see Gustave Reynier, *Le Roman sentimental avant l' "Astrée"* (Paris, A. Colin, 1908), pp. 14, 271–277; and Magendie, *Le Roman français*, p. 142.

is aware of what went on in a sinking ship from which there were no survivors. Unlike overt fiction, pseudohistory cannot provide intimate knowledge of the characters' thoughts and emotions without resort to such awkward and constricting devices as autobiographical report or the discovery of a collection of letters. If the imposture is successful, the author loses credit for his achievement, except perhaps among an intimate circle made privy to the secret.

The handicaps of pseudohistory did not go unrecognized. A defender of Scudéry's *Clélie* prefers fictional portraits of a character to historical ones because the latter are only "halfedrawn;" they can "afford us very little knowledge how generous his deportment was in conversation; and amongst his Friends, how nobly he loved or hated; and how tender a relation, or faithful friend, he shewed himself in all the diversities of adventures."[51] Avoidance of the appearance of fiction also demands the abandonment of the traditional poetic devices. Since truth is artless, rude verity must be preferable to polished falsehood, and indeed, when sweet Zephyrus rises from his fragrant bed and calls forth lovely Flora from her chamber, the reader finds it difficult to believe that he is hearing a tale about things that have happened. Even the great Aristotelian principle of the unity of action must be sacrificed on the altar of verity. As the encyclopedist Bayle says, since booksellers and authors know that love intrigues and similar adventures please more when they are believed to be real, "the new Romances keep as far off as possible from the Romantick Way," the way, that is, of the heroic poem in prose.[52]

Furetière makes mock of the "Romantick Way" in *Le Roman bourgeois* (1666): "Je chante les amours et les advantures de plusieurs bourgeois de Paris, de l'un et de l'autre sexe; et ce qui est de plus merveilleux, c'est que je les chante, et si je ne sçay

51. Scudéry, *Clelia, an excellent new Romance*, IV (1677), preface by the translator G. H.
52. Bayle, *An Historical and Critical Dictionary*, s.v. "Nidhard."

pas la musique."[53] He will not invoke the Muses nor begin *in medias res;* nor will he concern himself with heroes and heroines and elaborate descriptions of the scene. He is unable to comment on the emotional response of Nicodème to the sight of Javotte because there was nobody present to feel the young man's pulse.[54] At the beginning of the second book of *Le Roman bourgeois* he calls that reader a fool who expects it to be linked to the first. Such links are easy enough to invent in heroic or fabulous poems where the author can do what he pleases, but it is a different matter in an account "tres-veritable et tres-sincere" such as this to which he has given only the form, without in any way changing the substance. The reader must therefore not suppose that the book will end with the marriage of the various couples—some will have had enough of love, others will marry secretly, and of still others the reporter will have had no knowledge. Such unity as may be found in his book, Furetière concludes, the binder of its pages will provide.[55]

Furetière's mockery is double-edged, for he ridicules not only romancers *à la Scudéry* but also those who would pass their fictions off as truth without recognizing the limitations that truth-telling inevitably imposes. One who pretends to be a historian cannot at the same time claim credit for inventing his matter. He may indeed cleanse the account which he has received of Newgate language and suppress what might be upsetting to gentle readers. He may comment morally and philosophically on the course of events. He may even give some form to the story provided that his editing does not alter the facts. But he must deny himself that god-like title of "maker" by which Sidney glorified the work of the poet.

Such self-denial is not characteristic of imaginative authors.

53. Antoine Furetière, *Le Roman bourgeois,* in *Romanciers du XVIIᵉ siècle,* ed. A. Adam (Paris, Gallimard, 1958), p. 903.
54. *Ibid.,* p. 908.
55. *Ibid.,* p. 1025.

Whether for that reason, or because sophisticated readers remained skeptical despite the efforts made to convince them, protestations of the truth of stories are sometimes made with what amounts to a disarming wink. Sorel raises the question as to whether Francion was really a certain gentleman whose biography his friend Du Parc undertook to write, only to put it aside with, "Mais cela n'importe de rien, Il suffit que nous reconnoissons l'excellence du livre."[56] Defoe's assertion that he believes *Robinson Crusoe* to be "a just history of fact" is tempered by the addendum "neither is there any appearance of fiction in it" and by the suggestion that, in any case, the reader will be both diverted and instructed.[57] In early editions of *Pamela* and *Clarissa Harlowe* Richardson describes himself as merely the editor of collections of letters, but in the Preface to *Sir Charles Grandison* he writes, "How such remarkable Collections of private Letters fell into [the editor's] hands he hopes the Reader will not think it very necessary to inquire."[58] Because the question of historical truth is left open, the reader is kept, on the one hand, from denouncing the "editor" as a liar, and, on the other, from rejecting the story outright as a figment of the imagination (though, if he is at all knowledgable, he must know that it is just that). Richardson makes the point in a letter to Bishop Warburton in which he explains that he is reluctant to use the Preface which the Bishop has written for *Clarissa* because it treats that story explicitly as a fiction: "Will you, good Sir, allow me to mention, that I could wish that the *Air* of Genuiness had been kept up, tho' I want not the Letters to be *thought* genuine; only so far kept up, I mean, as that they should not prefatically be owned *not* to be genuine: and this for fear of weakening their Influence where

56. Charles Sorel, preface to *Francion*, edition of 1633, in *Romanciers*, ed. Adam, p. 1269.
57. Alan Dugald McKillop, *The Early Masters of English Fiction* (Lawrence, University of Kansas Press, 1956), p. 39.
58. *Ibid.*, p. 42.

any of them are aimed to be exemplary; as well as to avoid hurting that kind of Historical Faith which Fiction itself is generally read with, tho' we know it to be Fiction."[59] What Richardson seems to seek for his story is an acceptance only a shade different from that of the Middle Ages for the apocryphal tales: they could not be warranted as true, but they might be true, and in any case could be read without danger to the soul, perhaps with profit.

Although in the early editions of his novels Richardson clung to the modest role of "editor," he was proud of his power of invention, even to the point of denying it to his rival Fielding. After remarking in a letter to Mrs. Donellan that Fielding's characters are representations, little altered, of the author himself, his first wife, and his acquaintances, Richardson continues, "His brawls, his jarrs, his gaols, his spunging-houses, are all drawn from what he has seen and known. As I said (witness also his hamper plot) he has little or no invention."[60] It is odd to find such criticism from one who had publicly asserted that he invented nothing whatever.

Richardson's denial of the power of invention to Fielding points to a way of making stories that evades the distinction between fact and fancy and so allows the author to claim that he is both telling the truth and creating something new. He does not fill historical blanks with "conjectures," mingle fiction with history, write history under a veil, or falsely protest that his fictions are true. Rather, he draws his characters, situations, and actions from his observation of the world as it is, and modifies and arranges these ingredients to suit his artistic purpose. His "portraits" are of real people, perhaps somewhat altered and under feigned names; the events correspond to real happenings. The result is a kind of narrative not envisaged by Sidney and the Renaissance defenders of fiction, for the mat-

59. *Ibid.*
60. *Novel and Romance*, ed. Williams, pp. 174–175.

ter is not what may be and should be (whether or not it has been) but what has indeed been. Furetière's tale of Lucrece in the first book of *Le Roman bourgeois* is of this nature. The preface announces that it is a fiction, but not, as the reader might expect, a *roman à clef:* it is futile to look for the key because the wards have been confused, and, if the reader begins to think that he recognizes the portrait of someone whom he knows, he will soon find the character acting like somebody else. The story of a bourgeois maid who was cheated of her virginity by a smooth gentleman's promise of marriage is nevertheless true in the sense that the thing has certainly happened. It may not be historically true that the maid was such a maid and the man such a man, that the circumstances and sequence of events were those described by the author. But since the characters and the actions are recognizably those we see daily, the story proved so effective, the preface declares, as to warn a real young woman from such an unfortunate experience.[61] This claim of truth to things as they are, truth to "life," becomes a principal defense of fictional narrative. If an author's invention is challenged, he responds by pointing to the world of fact. The question as to whether or not an imagined man may explode by spontaneous combustion is no longer one of plausibility, probability, or verisimilitude but of history: if such a thing happened, the novelist may make use of it. His fiction is no fantasy but a composition of true occurrences and real people; his matter comes not from his imagination but from his notebook.

But the old dilemma remains. Although writers of fiction continued, during the eighteenth century and after, to pretend more or less earnestly that they were really historians, only the altogether naïve, like Lady Arabella in *The Female Quixote*, took them at their word or damned them as liars. Increasing familiarity with the novel and its separation from history both

61. *Romanciers,* ed. Adam, p. 901.

in style and on the shelves of bookshops identified the form and gave it recognition. The audience had come to accept such stories, not as perhaps true but rather with that willing suspension of disbelief of which Coleridge writes. It was agreed that narrative fictions might entertain and teach moral lessons (or immoral ones) and that the more "true to life" they were the more effective their teaching. Yet the difference between truth to life and historical truth continued to plague and to challenge "poets" and their defenders. There seems to be a persistent reluctance to accept the artistic composition of verities as equivalent to the representation of verity, even such inadequate representation as lies within the power of a historian. A few examples must suffice to show the continuing uncertainty and defensiveness of nineteenth-century novelists as to the validity of their vocation. Hawthorne imagines his Puritan ancestors commenting on his novel writing: "What is he? murmurs one gray shadow of my forefathers to the other. A writer of story-books! What kind of a business in life,— what mode of glorifying God, or being serviceable to mankind in his day and generation,—may that be? Why the degenerate fellow might as well have been a fiddler!"[62] Manzoni realizes that man's most rational appetite for the relation of facts exercises a fascination for him which results in his rejection as puerile of intermixed invention. He therefore proposes to write a story which will represent a particular condition of society by means of actions and characters so like the truth that they may be taken as true history just come to light. Like Furetière, but in all seriousness, he rejects artistic unity as incompatible with real life, and expresses the hope that criticism will come to see it as a defect rather than as a virtue.[63]

62. Hawthorne, "The Custom-House," introduction to *The Scarlet Letter.*
63. See the letters to Fauriel quoted in the introduction by Natalino Sapegno to Manzoni, *I promessi sposi* (Milan, Feltrinelli, 1964), pp. xiii, xxi.

For Henry James, it is intolerable that a novelist should admit that his story is make-believe: "It implies that the novelist is less occupied in looking for the truth (the truth, of course I mean, that he assumes, the premises that we must grant him, whatever they may be) than the historian, and in doing so it deprives him at a stroke of all his standing-room. To represent and illustrate the past, the actions of men, is the task of either writer, and the only difference that I can see is, in proportion as he succeeds, to the honour of the novelist, consisting as it does in his having more difficulty in collecting his evidence, which is so far from being purely literary."[64]

The novelist's demand for "standing-room," his touchiness about the charge of frivolity, his refusal to accept the modest role of maker of make-believe, his search for an art which denies itself, his fudging of the question of fictional truth, and his effort to identify his task with that of the historian or to claim superiority in the competition are all inheritances of the dilemma of the storytellers of the sixteenth and seventeenth centuries. And the persistence of that dilemma is made evident by current experiments ranging from "novels" which can be advertised as historically true in every particular to those which, in the attempt to capture a reality beyond reach of the historians, abandon not only the ancient art of the heroic poem but even sequential narrative and coherence.

64. Henry James, "The Art of Fiction," in *Selected Literary Criticism: Henry James*, ed. Morris Shapira (New York, Horizon Press, 1964), p. 51. See also Joseph Conrad, "Henry James, an Appreciation," in *Notes on Life and Letters* (Garden City, N.Y., Doubleday, 1921), p. 17.

INDEX